Devil's Advocates

DEVIL'S ADVOCATES is a series of books devoted to exploring the classics of horror cinema. Contributors to the series come from the fields of teaching, academia, journalism and fiction, but all have one thing in common: a passion for the horror film and a desire to share it with the widest possible audience.

'The admirable Devil's Advocates series is not only essential – and fun – reading for the serious horror fan but should be set texts on any genre course.'
Dr Ian Hunter, Reader in Film Studies, De Montfort University, Leicester

'Auteur Publishing's new Devil's Advocates critiques on individual titles... offer bracingly fresh perspectives from passionate writers. The series will perfectly complement the BFI archive volumes.' **Christopher Fowler,** *Independent on Sunday*

'Devil's Advocates has proven itself more than capable of producing impassioned, intelligent analyses of genre cinema... quickly becoming the go-to guys for intelligent, easily digestible film criticism.' *Horror Talk.com*

'Auteur Publishing continue the good work of giving serious critical attention to significant horror films.' *Black Static*

 DevilsAdvocatesbooks

DevilsAdBooks

ALSO AVAILABLE IN THIS SERIES

A Girl Walks Home Alone at Night Farshid Kazemi
Black Sunday Martyn Conterio
The Blair Witch Project Peter Turner
Blood and Black Lace Roberto Curti
The Blood on Satan's Claw David Evans-Powell
Candyman Jon Towlson
Cannibal Holocaust Calum Waddell
Cape Fear Rob Daniel
Carrie Neil Mitchell
The Company of Wolves James Gracey
The Conjuring Kevin J. Wetmore Jr.
Creepshow Simon Brown
Cruising Eugenio Ercolani & Marcus Stiglegger
The Curse of Frankenstein Marcus K. Harmes
Daughters of Darkness Kat Ellinger
Dawn of the Dead Jon Towlson
Dead of Night Jez Conolly & David Bates
The Descent James Marriot
The Devils Darren Arnold
Don't Look Now Jessica Gildersleeve
The Evil Dead Lloyd Haynes
The Fly Emma Westwood
Frenzy Ian Cooper
Halloween Murray Leeder
House of Usher Evert Jan van Leeuwen
In the Mouth of Madness Michael Blyth
It Follows Joshua Grimm

Ju-on The Grudge Marisa Hayes
Let the Right One In Anne Billson
M Samm Deighan
Macbeth Rebekah Owens
The Masque of the Red Death Steve Haberman
The Mummy Doris V. Sutherland
Nosferatu Cristina Massaccesi
The Omen Adrian Schober
Peeping Tom Kiri Bloom Walden
Possession Alison Taylor
Re-Animator Eddie Falvey
Repulsion Jeremy Carr
Saw Benjamin Poole
Scream Steven West
The Shining Laura Mee
Shivers Luke Aspell
The Silence of the Lambs Barry Forshaw
Suspiria Alexandra Heller-Nicholas
The Texas Chain Saw Massacre James Rose
The Thing Jez Conolly
Trouble Every Day Kate Robertson
Twin Peaks: Fire Walk With Me Lindsay Hallam
Witchfinder General Ian Cooper

FORTHCOMING

The Cabin in the Woods Susanne Kord
IT: Chapters 1 & 2 Alissa Burger
Pet Sematary Shellie McMurdo

Devil's Advocates

Snuff

Mark McKenna

Acknowledgements

Thanks to Martin Shingler and Yannis Tzioumakis, who were both kind enough to offer feedback on earlier drafts of this book. I would like to thank José Arroyo, whose podcast first alerted me to the work of Joaquín Aras, and to Aras himself, for our conversations and for granting permission to reprint images of his work. Thanks go to Sharon Coleclough, Neil Jackson, Steve Jones, Gary Needham and Johnny Walker for their support in the development of this book, and to the staff of the Albert Sloman Library, at the University of Essex for supporting my requests to view the archives of the National Viewers' and Listeners' Association. Thanks also go to Katie Gallof and Bloomsbury Publishing, who published an earlier version of Chapter 3, which appeared in *Snuff: Real Death and Screen Media* (2016). This reworked version appears here with permission. My thanks to John Atkinson at Auteur/LUP for his support and flexibility while I was writing this book, and finally, my apologies always to my wife, Sarah and my son, Eli and my daughter Meg. May you never let me forget!

First published in 2022 by
Auteur, an imprint of
Liverpool University Press,
4 Cambridge Street,
Liverpool
L69 7ZU

Series design: Nikki Hamlett at Cassels Design
Set by Cassels Design, Luton UK

All rights reserved. No part of this publication may be reproduced in any material form (including photocopying or storing in any medium by electronic means and whether or not transiently or incidentally to some other use of this publication) without the permission of the copyright owner.

An earlier version of the material in Chapter 3 was published in *Snuff: Real Death and Screen Media* (ed. Neil Jackson, 2016). Thanks to Bloomsbury for their permission to rework this material.

British Library Cataloguing-in-Publication Data
A catalogue record for this book is available from the British Library

ISBN paperback: 978-1-800-85939-5
ISBN hardback: 978-1-800-85938-8
ISBN PDF: 978-1-800-85854-1

Contents

A Note on this Research 7

Introduction 9

Chapter 1. The Creation of *Snuff* 15

Chapter 2. The Origins of *Snuff* 33

Chapter 3. The Authenticity of *Snuff* 45

Chapter 4. The Legacy of *Snuff* 61

Chapter 5. The Reality and the Redefinition of *Snuff* 77

Conclusion 93

Bibliography 97

Filmography 107

Figures

Fig. 1. Screenshots from Shackleton's coda to *Snuff* (© August Films/Selected Pictures).

Fig. 2. 'Blood Money': *Snuff* nets $59,912 in the first six days (author's own collection © Monarch Releasing Corporation).

Fig. 3. 'Boycott Mann Theatres': Women Against Violence Against Women flyer.

Fig. 4. Protests outside of the National Theatre on the release of *Snuff* (from the 'Does Snuff Exist?' episode of the Channel 4 series *The Dark Side of Porn*, 2006).

Fig. 5. *Body of a Female* (1964) poster (© Amlay Pictures).

Fig. 6. 'Wall-to-Wall Gore': Astra Video's horror double-bill (author's own collection).

Fig. 7. *Snuff* video sleeves, black- and blue-sleeved variants (blue variant © Astra Video Ltd.).

Fig. 8. *Snuff* video shop poster (© Astra Video Ltd.).

Fig. 9. 'Snuff Movies' (Anon.), from the archives of the National Viewers' and Listeners' Association, Albert Sloman Library, University of Essex.

Fig 10. *Snuff 1976*, video installation and sound remake of *Snuff*, Joaquín Aras, 83 minutes, 2015. The project was supported by the Bienal de Arte Joven de Buenos Aires.

A Note on this Research

As one might expect given the nature of this book there are detailed descriptions of murder throughout, and while some of these descriptions are drawn from the textual analysis of narrative cinema, many of these are descriptions of real murders, with accounts drawn from press press discourse and legal transcripts. There is a tendency both within the press, but also within legal frameworks governing extreme material, to conflate quite horrific murders with pornography making research of this kind fraught with legal and ethical issues.

In 2008 the British Government added a clause to the Criminal Justice and Immigration Act criminalising a range of sexual and violent material under the banner of extreme pornography (for an example of material that presented legal issues see Smith, 2016). Under the provision of the Act, imagery can be categorised as extreme if it is considered to be 'grossly offensive, disgusting or otherwise of an obscene character'. Aside from the inherent difficulties in reaching a consensus about what 'offensive', 'disgusting' or 'obscene' material might look like, the Act stipulates that pornography will be considered 'extreme' if it portrays in an explicit and realistic way any of the following —

(a) an act which threatens a person's life,

(b) an act which results, or is likely to result, in serious injury to a person's anus, breasts or genitals,

(c) an act which involves sexual interference with a human corpse, or

(d) a person performing an act of intercourse or oral sex with an animal (whether dead or alive).

While necrophilia and bestiality would no doubt feature in most definitions of 'offensive', 'disgusting' or 'obscene', the fact that this legislation extends to fictional representations means that, in practice, if a reasonable person looking at the image would think that the person or animal was real, then that would be sufficient to warrant prosecution. Alongside this, subsection (b) effectively criminalises a whole range of sexual related to BDSM, irrespective of individual consent.

However, leaving issues of consent and the subjective assessments of what might constitute 'extreme' material to one side, the Act presents numerous difficulties for anyone who would research material of this kind. In 2009, and in response to the introduction of the legislation, Steve Jones and Sharif Mowlabocus detailed some of the legal and ethical implications of the Act on researchers whose interests lie in material that 'blur[s] boundaries between porn and horror', or that which is otherwise known as extreme pornography (2009: 613). They highlight that unless researchers are attached to a particular project with permissions granted to view prohibited material, individual academics are not immune from prosecution should they choose to access materials that contravene this legislation.

While this book is primarily concerned with depictions of murder, the frequent conflation of pornography and horror means that it is valuable to ground my own practice as a researcher within established research principles and methodological approaches. And while this book takes the film *Snuff* as its starting point, it is equally interested in how the idea of the snuff movie spread, the role that the 1976 film played in that dissemination, and how the established definition of what constitutes a snuff movie may be out of step with contemporary society. This shift in emphasis from a book that is explicitly focussed on the film itself, to an expanded notion that considers the cultural mythology of the snuff movie, means that the book must consider crimes of sexual abuse, bestiality and cannibalism, and films that are understandably illegal. However, because of the broad cultural focus of the book, it is more important that this work accurately reflects the discourse that surrounds these crimes, than it is that this material is drawn from my own primary accounts. In these instances, descriptions of the footage are secondary and drawn largely from press discourse, whereas material that is pornographic but does not contravene Section 63 of the Criminal Justice and Immigration Act, is the result of my own primary analysis.

Introduction

Few films in the history of cinema have inspired the kind of legacy that follows Michael and Roberta Findlay's 1976 film, *Snuff*. Originally scheduled for release in 1971 as *The Slaughter*, the film lay gathering dust for five years until Allan Shackleton, a savvy New York distributor who was known primarily for pornography, saw an opportunity to capitalise on the rumour that films featuring footage of real murder were arriving in the United States from South America. Shackleton added a newly filmed conclusion onto the Findlays' long forgotten film and coupled it with a hyperbolic advertising campaign that ensured that the film would never be forgotten again. In doing so, Shackleton gave credence to the rumours that snuff movies were real and although it was quickly debunked as little more than a publicity stunt, the film's very existence has ensured that the myth of the snuff movie has not only survived but has prospered, continuing to reverberate throughout popular culture.

Alexandra Heller-Nicholas has argued that while *Snuff* might not be the 'best' film produced in the 1970s, it could be the decade's most important 'worst' film (2009); proof perhaps that an idea can often be more powerful than its execution. After all, the power of *Snuff* comes not from the quality of its production, and not from the sophistication of its special effects, but from its central conceit – from the belief that somewhere, at some time, someone was killed on camera, and that this murder was carried out for commercial gain and for the sexual gratification of a debased and deviant audience. Indeed, so pervasive was the belief in the existence of snuff movies that in the wake of the film's release the Federal Bureau of Investigation (FBI) formed a special division dedicated to finding and prosecuting those responsible. They found nothing. But in the course of their investigation, they did establish the parameters of what a legitimate snuff movie might look like, if and when it was found. FBI Agent Ken Lanning suggests that in order to qualify as a legitimate snuff movie, the representation would need to be:

i. A visual depiction of murder (this can be either a series of photographs or a video)

ii. This imagery must have been produced to sexually arouse its intended audience

iii. This imagery must then be commercially distributed for financial gain.

These criteria have become the defining characteristics of the snuff movie, which Lanning compares to the search for the Holy Grail, 'much talked about, long sought after, but never found' (Barry, 2006).

In 1976, many believed that the film *Snuff* fulfilled all of the criteria of the snuff movie, though in retrospect this is difficult to understand why, especially when considering how poorly executed the conclusion to the film is. However, that does not mean that there are not important things to be said about the film, or its place in history. The film popularised an idea that has had a lasting effect on cinema and popular culture more generally and it is because of the impact of the concept that, unlike most other contributions to the Devil's Advocates series, this book moves away from the absolute focus of a single film to also consider the cultural impact of that concept and the ways in which the film contributed to the dissemination of the idea. Because of this broader focus, the book is ostensibly structured in chronological order, tracking the concept as it reverberates through popular culture and facilitating a discussion that explores the cultural impact that comes from the recognition of the concept. However, rather than begin with the emergence of the snuff myth, Chapter One 'The Creation of *Snuff*', instead begins with the creation of the titular film. As this book will demonstrate, the film arguably did more to popularise belief in the snuff movie than any of the speculative reports that had appeared in the press in the run up to its release. Because of that, this chapter foregrounds its importance. Beginning with an exploration of the production of *The Slaughter*, the chapter explores the production, distribution and exhibition of Shackleton's *Snuff*, providing a detailed overview of its narrative, but also exploring how the film capitalised on the already existing myth of the snuff movie in order to mobilise a media furore as a low-cost marketing device. It considers how this furore helped to amplify the myth of the snuff movie and consolidate an idea that has prospered, even now almost fifty years later. Chapter Two considers the industrial and cultural contexts that gave rise to the film in the first place, exploring the ongoing relationship between snuff and 'the Manson Family', before exploring how shifts in the regulation of film in the United States contributed to an environment in which the production of a film like *Snuff* was almost inevitable. Chapter Three considers an element that is fundamental to the success of the snuff myth, the debate as to the authenticity of the film. However, rather than revisit the well-trodden historical debates about whether the film contains footage of a real murder (it doesn't!), this chapter will instead refocus those ideas onto a secondary debate that exists and that is unique to the United Kingdom. *Snuff* had been scheduled for release in 1982, when it became caught up in the 'video nasties' moral panic. The likelihood of prosecution meant that the distributor tried to distance themselves from the release, leaving a question mark hanging over the provenance of the version that did finally make it to market. This chapter will explore the debates around the video release of *Snuff*, considering the arguments that persist about the authenticity and legitimacy of the video and what is at stake for collectors when they engage in these debates. Chapter Four examines the cultural legacy of the film, tracing the effect that the film had upon the myth and the effect that the myth has had upon society. While primarily focussed upon the Anglo/American reception to the myth, this chapter will also consider the cultural legacy of the film in South America, exploring the political implications of Shackleton's decision to remove the end sequence from the film, and in doing so remove any reference to the actors who had performed in *The Slaughter*. Finally, Chapter Five, moves discussion away from the absolute focus of the film and legacy of the film, to instead explore some of the most horrific crimes of recent years. It will consider how each has been discursively constructed as evidence of the snuff movie, and will explore how one film, *I Lunatic I Icepick*, presents the most credible challenge to the mythical status of the snuff movie. Over the course of Chapter Five, it will consider the market that exists for extreme imagery online and explore the motivations to both watch and produce material of this kind.

This is not the first book to have been written about snuff movies. Indeed, since the early 1990s, there has been much interest in the subject, with notable works coming both from within the academy and aimed at a wider audience. David Kerekes and David Slater's book, *Killing for Culture: An Illustrated History of Death on Film from Mondo to Snuff*, is, without doubt, the most important example of the latter. First released in 1994, and then in a revised edition in 2016, *Killing for Culture* is a forensic study of death in film and established many of the known facts about the release of *Snuff*. In 2015, Stephen Milligen published *The Bloodiest Thing That Ever Happened in Front of a Camera: Conservative Politics, 'Porno Chic' and Snuff*, a densely researched book that details the political afterlife of the film in an American context.

Outside of the popular press, scholarly interest in *Snuff* predates these works by a number of years. Linda Williams explored the relationship between *Snuff* and sadomasochistic pornographies as early as 1989, concluding that both *Snuff* the film and snuff the idea 'exist[s] at the contradictory intersection between the spectacles of pleasure (generally assumed to be real in hard-core pornography), and pain (generally assumed to be faked in horror films)', and that 'the genre mistake that read *Snuff*'s violent horror as pornography and therefore as real demonstrates the need to be very clear about what kinds of violence and what kinds of perversions do operate in contemporary hard-core commercial pornography" (1989: 42). Eithne Johnson and Eric Schaefer explore the wider implications of the distributor collapsing these genres in their 1993 article 'Soft Core/Hard Gore: *Snuff* as a Crisis in Meaning'. Here they suggest that because *Snuff* defied easy categorisation, it 'exposed deep divides within society regarding "high," "middle," and "low" cultural forms and definitions of taste', going on to chart the mobilisation of the snuff myth as a means of shifting the definition of pornography from that of purely sexual representation to footage that is ostensibly violent (1993: 41). Also in 1993, Avedon Carol offered a challenge to the feminist hyperbole that had conflated pornography and violence suggesting that it was 'virtually impossible to have a reasoned discussion of actual pornography without firmly insisting that the "feminist" definition be dismissed' (1993: 126).

All of these chapters are in some way concerned with ideas of what might constitute the real, and it this question that continued to preoccupy later work. Much of this is interested in the idea that a real murder was committed in the conclusion to *Snuff*, while some of it neatly challenges those perspectives through analysis of the aesthetics of that representation. In 2000, Julian Petley highlighted that the belief that someone had actually died on camera in the conclusion to *Snuff* was ludicrous, not least because the sequence is filmed in Classical Hollywood style, 'complete with alternating point-of-view shots' (2000: 207). Petley documents the passage of the myth in the United Kingdom through the British press and the place of *Snuff* in the 'video nasties' moral panic. In a later article, Petley examines how another 'video nasty', *Cannibal Holocaust* (1980), contributed to the snuff myth by famously blurring the lines between the real and the simulated by juxtaposing the killing of real animals with the dramatized murder of people (2005). Petley argues that this collision trampled on the carefully erected and culturally sanctioned distinctions between fictional and factual modes of representing death.

In 2009, Alexandra Heller-Nicholas wrote an important article examining the role of 'June', a third, and often overlooked figure in the coda to *Snuff*, who holds down the victim while the director disembowels her. Then, in 2014, Heller-Nicholas revisited *Snuff* with *Found Footage Horror Films: Fear and the Appearance of Reality*, exploring the emergence of the found-footage genre and its relationship to the snuff myth. Steve Jones has written extensively on the blurring distinctions between pornography and horror and the ways in which this juxtaposition can often reflect serious and complicated philosophical ideas. In 2011 he wrote 'Dying to be Seen: Snuff-Fiction's Problematic Fantasies of "Reality"' that explored the faux-snuff film, its interest in sexual violence and how the form balanced issues of fantasy with an aesthetic that relied on notions of authenticity. In 2016, Jones, Kerekes and Petley contributed chapters to Neil Jackson, Shaun Kimber, Johnny Walker and Thomas Joseph Watson's edited collection *Snuff: Real Death and Screen Media* (which also features an earlier version of Chapter Three: 'The Authenticity of Snuff'). The chapters were drawn from what was believed to be world's first academic conference devoted to the cultural mythology of the snuff film in an edited collection that presented fifteen case studies that each explored the persistence of the myth from different perspectives. Outside of these many contributions, there are as many chapters and articles that have explored individual films, or series of films that have capitalised on, and contributed to, the snuff myth (see Jackson, 2003; Kimber, 2014; Walker, 2016 among others). However, despite the extensive academic work that has been done around *Snuff* and its relationship to the snuff myth, there has never been a sole-authored monograph from within the academy that consolidates all of the work to date. This book will draw upon all of these works, but also upon the source material that informs these works to present a historiography of both *Snuff* the film, and snuff the myth, in a synthesis that seeks to reassess this material and offer new ways of thinking about *Snuff*.

Chapter 1. The Creation of *Snuff*

As the first commercial film to capitalise on the myth of the snuff movie, *Snuff* occupies a unique place in cinematic history. And although the myth of the snuff movie did not begin with the release of the film, the film's existence has only served to consolidate the belief that somewhere, at some time, someone was killed on camera, in an attack that was as much about the sexual gratification of the film's intended audience as it was about the commercial rewards for those producing the film. In the United Kingdom, the persistence of the snuff myth has only been exacerbated by the fact that the film was only ever briefly available, banned under the Obscene Publications Act (1959) in the events that led to the introduction of the Video Recordings Act in 1984. While the film is no longer banned (having been certificated for general release by the British Board of Film Classification in 2003) and is now even available to rent via Amazon Prime, prior to digital download the film had still yet to receive a legitimate physical release.

However, it could be argued that this has only benefitted the reputation of the film, for, had the film been widely seen upon its release, it would have certainly only served to undermine any belief in the myth of real murder. Although the film's marketing campaign promised 'the bloodiest thing that ever happened in front of a camera', for many the film is regarded as a 'tedious' (Lyons, 2019) and 'ineptly staged' (Inglis, 2018) exploitation 'quickie' that is mired in manufactured controversy. Nevertheless, it is exactly this manufactured controversy that has ensured that the myth of real murder has persisted unabated, guaranteeing that *Snuff* will likely remain the best known least seen movie of all time. This chapter will examine the production, distribution, and exhibition of *Snuff* in the United States, considering how it's initial reception of the film continues to inform the popular imagination and shape our understanding of the snuff movie.

Producing *The Slaughter*

Snuff began life as a low-budget and little-seen American exploitation film called *The Slaughter*, produced in Argentina in 1970 by the husband-and-wife team, Michael and Roberta Findlay. The Findlays had made their name producing sadomasochistic exploitation films and *The Slaughter* was an attempt to combine these elements into a commercial property that capitalised on the notoriety of 'the Manson Family' murders that had dominated the headlines throughout 1970 and early 1971. *The Slaughter* was filmed on a budget of $30,000, 100 miles north of Buenos Aries, Argentina, with funds raised by backers that included doctors and dentists (Nolte, c.1987: 4-5). The investors were attracted by the glamour of being attached to a film and firmly believed that shooting in South America made sound financial sense (Abel, 1975: 36). Shot over a period of four weeks, the film was based upon a script that was developed by Michael Findlay that incorporated a confused political subtext into its narrative. He believed that in order to interest the backers, he and his wife needed to offer something different from their usual fare. To that end, he developed *The Slaughter* as a commentary on the numerous reports that high-ranking Nazi officials had escaped prosecution for their crimes by hiding out in South America – Adolph Eichmann, the notorious architect of Hitler's 'Final Solution', and Dr Josef Mengele, the infamous 'Angel of Death' who conducted bizarre experiments on the men, women and children held at the Auschwitz death camp, were among those who had fled to South America. Findlay felt that if his film could incorporate some of this subtext into the narrative it would then offer a greater political commentary and would therefore stand a greater chance of success. He was wrong. Roberta would later comment that the politics of the film were very confused and presented the Manson-like figure as a kind of avenging angel, killing Nazis who had escaped to South America while asking wasn't it 'the same thing as the Israelis supplying guns to the Arabs?' (Peary, 1978: 30). Despite the confusing political subtext, the script proved popular with the investors who believed that the violence and the exotic locations would ensure that the film was a box office success (Peary, 1978: 30). The production manager cast the model and former Miss International beauty pageant winner, Mirta Teresita Massa in the lead role, and they hired a mansion and shot there for a week in 1970.

In many respects, *The Slaughter* could be read as a progressive if poorly executed film that mashes together the already established sub-genre of the female biker movie (seen in films like *She-Devils On Wheels* [1968] and *The Girl On A Motorcycle* [1968]) with the emerging subgenre of the satanic cult movie, a genre that would be popularised as the '70s progressed, with films like *Race with the Devil* (1975) and *The Devil's Rain* (1975). However, stylistically, the film owes its greatest debt to the genre-defining youth movie

Easy Rider (1969), a film that had been released two years earlier, and that informs much of the aesthetic of *The Slaughter*. So great is this debt that the film opens with a sequence of two female hippy bikers riding tandem to a soundtrack that mimics Steppenwolf's iconic anthem 'Born to be Wild'. In case there was any doubt surrounding the inference, this footage is then intercut with footage of the rest of the gang smoking marijuana and snorting cocaine. It is here that we are introduced to the (apparently) charismatic cult leader, Satán (pronounced Sah-tan), whom we learn is the leader of the all-girl gang of bikers. However, without the budget, or indeed the talent that was assembled to produce *Easy Rider*, the film was bound to fail.

The narrative, though often confusing and difficult to follow, sees Massa's character, the actress Terry London, and her producer, Max Marsh, arriving at Chile's Arturo Merino Benítez International Airport. They are greeted by reporters who want to know whether the rumours that they are to be wed while they are visiting South America are true. They ask whether London will appear naked in the film that they are making together, but Marsh dismisses their enquiries, and the couple leave in a car that is waiting for them. When they arrive at the hotel, it becomes clear that London and Marsh are in a relationship, but when she refuses his advances and he leaves, we learn that she is also involved with another man, Horst Frank. London had met Frank in Long Island and hoped to reunite while she was visiting South America. She rings him and arranges to meet, much to the disappointment of Frank's guest, Angelica, who we later learn is an agent of Satán. She had been sent to Frank's house in the hope that she could seduce him, and then bear his child which would then be sacrificed in a Satanic ceremony. However, on learning that London is in a relationship with Frank, Satán decides that she can bear the child and makes arrangements to dispose of Marsh. We learn that Frank's family are hugely wealthy German émigrés when he encourages London to quit working for Marsh and to come and live with him in Argentina. Fiercely protective of her independence, London refuses his offer.

Improbably soon afterwards London becomes pregnant with Frank's child and when she leaves Marsh with Angelica at the carnival he is murdered by Satán's gang leaving room for them to target Frank, London and, the primary target of their plan, their unborn child. When we are finally introduced to Frank's father, we learn that much of his wealth is derived from selling munitions to General Moshe Dayan, the former Defence Minister of

Israel, aiding the fight against their Arab neighbours. Much is made of the fact that Jewish Israelis would purchase munitions from an exiled German businessman, and Frank's father asks London 'does that make him (General Dayan) less of a butcher than, say, Eichmann?' The almost comedic camera zoom in on his face implies that there is a direct correlation between Horst's father and Eichmann, though this subplot is never fully developed. Satán enters the room accompanied by Angelica who has come to collect her belongings, and a heated exchange ensues in which Satán questions the ethics of Frank and men like him who would sell the knife, or guns in this case, to the 'butchers' in order to profit from war. Satán and Angelica leave, and many months pass until, in a speech to the gang, Satán says:

> The unborn human being grows larger in the womb every day. Five, six, seven months have passed, and now the time has come – time to strike and kill just to be born. I have waited long enough. The time has come for you, my girls, to kill them all. The time has come for slaughter.

When the women arrive at the mansion, Frank is entertaining another couple. The gang kill the husband and wife and tie Frank to a tree in imagery clearly inspired by the martyrdom of Saint Sebastian. Though it is not directly visible it seems as if they cut off his genitals with a straight razor and they then enter the house and go upstairs to find London in bed with Frank's father. He pleads with them, offering them money and a chance to escape on his private jet, but unmoved by these pleas, they shoot him in the chest. They ask London repeatedly, 'Is that his?', pointing to the unborn baby in her womb. When she finally answers, 'Yes', Angelica plunges the knife into her stomach, and shouts 'Well, then you two go and join him'. We can only assume that this was the finale to *The Slaughter*, though one might expect more to be made of the sacrifice of the unborn child. The allusions to the Manson Family murders and parallels between the film and the murder of Sharon Tate were far from subtle. However, despite (or because of) being in poor taste, as timely as the film was, it failed to find an audience.

Producing *Snuff*

It is unclear whether *The Slaughter* was ever distributed in its original form. Some sources claim that it received a limited theatrical release (Stine, 1999: 31), while others insist that the film was never seen theatrically (Kerekes and Slater, 2016). Certainly, Roberta Findlay's own account would suggest that the film was so bad that they were unable to find a buyer and that it languished gathering dust on Shackleton's shelves until 1976. In a 1978 interview, Findlay claimed that the couple took the film to California and almost secured a deal, but this was derailed when the Motion Picture Association of America (MPAA) intervened arguing that the film was disgusting. She believed that both the audience and the censor were simply unprepared for a film about Charles Manson, especially one that seemed to want to present him in a favourable light (Peary, 1978: 30).

It is likely that the film would have remained forgotten were it not for the work of distributor Allan Shackleton. Shackleton had made his name releasing sexploitation films and had previously handled Roberta Findlay's film *Rosebud* in 1972. However, by 1975, his company, Monarch Releasing Corporation, was looking to diversify its catalogue, as he felt that the market for erotica was beginning to slow with many cinemas simply refusing to screen X-rated material (Kerekes and Slater, 2016). In 1975, Monarch appointed Barry Glasser as director of promotion and publicity with Glasser heading up the promotional campaigns for three new films: *Revenge of Cheerleaders* (1976) starring a then-unknown David Hasselhoff; *Fantastic Invasion of Planet Earth* (1966), a reissue of a film that had previously been released as *The Bubble* in 1966; and *Snuff* (Cocchi, 1976). *Snuff* was Shackleton's masterstroke, released amid rumours that the New York City Police Department had confiscated a number of films that allegedly featured sequences of real murder (Bronstein, 2011: 85). Dick Brass, a reporter for the New York Post, was convinced that snuff movies were real and reported that films that featured real murder were entering the United States from South America, calling them 'the ultimate obscenity' (Brass, 1975a: 3, 15).

Buoyed by these rumours, Shackleton commissioned the director Simon Nuchtern to produce an alternative ending to *The Slaughter*, a sequence that was filmed in the studio of Carter Stevens on 29th Street in New York. Shackleton then paired the augmented print with a hyperbolic advertising campaign and, in doing so, ensured that the film would never be forgotten again. His approach was as simple as it was effective, and although it may have been crude in its execution, it would prove enough to catapult the five-year-old forgotten film into infamy. As the narrative of *The Slaughter* approaches its stilted conclusion with the murder of the actress playing Terry London, the camera would cut away to a mock-up of the set on which that final scene had just been filmed. Here, the audience would be presented with the image of the director and a production assistant discussing the scene, both apparently aroused by what they have just seen. They begin to kiss. However, when she objects to being filmed by the crew, the director suddenly becomes violent, threatening her with a knife. He enlists the help of another production assistant to help pin her down (see Heller-Nicholas [2019] for an exploration of the role of June) while he drags the knife across her shoulder. He cuts off her finger with pliers, before recruiting another member of the crew to take an electric saw and cut off the woman's hand at the wrist. This sequence reaches its bloody conclusion when the director plunges a knife into her stomach, disembowelling her and holding her intestines high above his head while he screams maniacally. The screen goes black, and as we hear the last of the film rattle through the camera the director says 'Shit! We ran out film'. His colleague asks 'Did you get it? Did you get it all?', to which he replies 'Yes'. There are no closing credits, the film simply ends. There are no logos of affiliates, or details of the cast and crew – all of the conventional signifiers that the film has concluded are missing, and instead the audience is left wondering whether what they just saw on the screen was real.

At least, that was the idea in principle. In practice, for anyone with more than a passing interest in, or rudimentary understanding of, the ways in which cinema is constructed, there are glaring anomalies that serve only to disrupt our belief that what is being presented to us on screen is real. The performances are laughingly unconvincing, particularly the actor who plays the director in the sequence, who is comically excessive. The moment that he holds the intestines above his head and screams is especially problematic, and although it is clearly meant to shock and disturb, it instead plays out as ludicrous. The victim's screams and her understated spluttering of blood are completely unconvincing as an authentic response to the apparently horrific attack that she is undergoing. However, any failures in their respective performances are rendered insignificant when considered alongside the lack of realism that comes from the special effects. The moment that the knife is dragged across her shoulder is deeply unconvincing. Her shirt becomes immediately drenched in blood, but the angle of the knife is never sufficient to really create the illusion that the blade has even entered her body, let alone produced the buckets of blood that are by now pooling on her shirt. Similarly, when they

Fig. 1

cut off her fingertip with the pliers and the blood begins to squirt, we see the hollow of a cheap rubber hand and the unnatural flexibility of rubber fingers that are losing their shape under the pressure of the actor holding them down. This effect is only amplified when they sever her hand, and the hollow of her arm is left as her dismembered hand continues to grasp for air. However, perhaps the least convincing of all of the special effects comes at the end of this sequence at the moment she is disembowelled. This sequence features a set-up that has now become a staple in the modern horror film and is a technique that is used to great effect in *Friday the 13th* (1980) with the death of Kevin Bacon and a sequence that is famously borrowed from Mario Bava's seminal 1971 giallo, *A Bay of Blood*. Here the body of the actor or actress is suspended beneath a bed while a dummy body stands in place of their own. With this in place, the actor's face can react in a manner appropriate to the attack that their character is undergoing while the dummy body is eviscerated. In *Snuff*, this conventional set-up is used as they cut open the stomach of the production assistant and then reach into the cavity to pull out the offal that was standing in place of human intestines. However, the angle that the actress is lying at is never quite right in relation to the body that is being presented as her own, ultimately undermining the sequence completely.

However, for all of its issues, the combination of Shackleton's savvy marketing campaign, and the sheer excesses of the sequence was 'evidence' enough of the existence of the hitherto mythical snuff movie, and this is the genius of Shackleton's approach; for those who wanted to believe, it didn't matter that the performances were stilted, that the special effects looked phoney, or that the film was clearly edited. The idea that it might be real was enough to amplify the belief that is was.

Exhibiting *Snuff*

David Kerekes and David Slater have argued that 'what Shackleton did when he tagged an unconvincing ending onto the Findlay's *Slaughter* was validate a myth', suggesting that 'the rumour that there had been snuff films entering America suddenly developed an identity: even if their existence had yet to be proven, this is what they looked like' (1994: 23). Shackleton had moved quickly in his bid to capitalise on the idea of the snuff movie. The coda to *The Slaughter* was shot, cut and the film was in cinemas by January 16, 1976. Reports of snuff movies entering the US from South America had only begun appearing in the New York press in the winter of 1975. By October these stories were gaining ground, with Sgt. Joseph Horman of New York's Organized Crime Bureau suggesting that his office was close to acquiring an 8mm print of a 'porno film where an actress is actually murdered on camera', and crucially, that this film was allegedly one of eight such films in circulation. Horman cited 'highly reliable' figures from New York's criminal underbelly who has assured him that, not only were these films real, but that you could pay see them in costly private shows (Anon, 1975: 1, 70). It was these reports that prompted Shackleton into action and by November, *The Independent Film Journal* was reporting that Monarch Releasing had acquired *Snuff*, a film that they described as a 'controversial Argentinian production concerning porno actresses who are brutally slaughtered on camera' (Anon, 1975a: 15). The film's campaign was limited but effective, crudely drawn artwork surrounded by straplines that proclaimed that not only was *Snuff* the 'bloodiest thing to ever happen in front of a camera' but also that it was a 'film that could only be made in South America… Where Life is CHEAP!' (emphasis in original). Unsurprisingly, the film garnered immediate attention with the Citizens for Decency, an

LA-based morality group, branding *Snuff* a 'vile, loathsome assault on all civilised standards of conduct' (Anon, 1975a: 15).

By December, *Variety* was reporting that Shackleton's *Snuff* was slated to premiere in Indianapolis followed by openings in New York and Los Angeles, and although the magazine was cynical about the likelihood that the film featured real murder, it was happy to speculate on what it might mean for screen violence if the film were indeed real. In interview, Shackleton was vague and evasive, suggesting that he was distributing the film for a producer whose name and nationality he refused to disclose. He also revealed that he had already been the target of several decency groups though he refused to name them (Jacobson, 1976: 4). His refusal piqued *Variety*'s interest, who followed up their article with an interview with Michael Findlay who had been told by a third party that *Snuff* was simply a reworking of his film *The Slaughter* and who suggested that there 'could be legal problems' for Shackleton if this did turn out to be the case. According to Findlay, a deal had been set with Joe Solomon of Fanfare Pictures, but that Solomon had backed out when the Motion Picture Association of America awarded the picture an X certificate (Anon, 1975b: 4). Nevertheless, and despite the potential legal issues, Shackleton assured exhibitors that 'all of the obstacles which might have stood in the way of the film's release have been removed' (Anon, 1975c 11), but before the film could even be screened, the promises of the advertising campaign landed Shackleton in hot water with the US Bureau of Customs who were concerned that the film violated federal statutes. The film was scrutinised thoroughly, though these agents were not interested in whether the murders committed on screen were real, only in whether the film had entered the country illegally, which, of course, it had not. Shackleton, almost triumphant, said that 'now that Customs have given us a green light, we anticipate no further legal difficulties and we intend to proceed with plans to distribute 'Snuff' throughout the country in the next few weeks' (Anon, 1976c: 3).

Despite receiving an incredible amount of free publicity, the premiere on January 16, 1976, at the Uptown Theatre in Indianapolis was a distinctly understated affair with less than two-dozen people in attendance, mostly law enforcement or members of the media. Even the posters in the lobby advertising the film were defaced with a hand-scrawled note assuring the audience that 'this is a theatrical presentation' and that 'no one was harmed or injured during filming' (Anon, 1976b: 18). While the film attracted a larger

Fig. 2

audience at its premiere in Wichita, Kansas, they were quick to label it fake with a local theatre spokesman commenting that 'a lot of people have been laughing instead of moaning' (Anon, 1976e: C-4). However, despite the film's initially poor performance and the indifferent responses that it was receiving elsewhere, by the time it arrived in Philadelphia in February, something had changed. Regency Theatre in Center City was picketed over two consecutive days by thirty-five women carrying placards. In turn, these demonstrations led to a refusal by daily newspapers to carry promotional adverts for the film and forced the exhibitor to move the screening from its first-run city centre cinema to the 61st Street Drive-In on the outskirts (Anon, 1976d: SE-4). When the film opened in Las Vegas it was only on condition that the theatre followed numerous rules laid out by City Attorney, Carl Lovell. Lovell had already been in contact with vice officers from Indianapolis, and although he was convinced that the film did not depict images of real murder, he argued that his office would invoke state laws on consumer protection should the theatre play along with Shackleton's ruse as to the authenticity of the murder (Anon, 1976f: 36). By the end of February, *Variety* was recording that, despite its mixed reception, *Snuff* was on course to be a profitable film, and that Michael Findlay and Shackleton had settled out-of-court for an undisclosed sum (Anon, 1976g: 22). While Findlay may have been pleased with his settlement after his film had languished gathering dust for so many years, it would appear that he settled too soon.

By the time the film opened in New York, either its reputation preceded it, or Shackleton had become more adept at drumming up publicity. Indeed, many attributed the early protests to Shackleton himself, with most accounts suggesting that he had recruited his own protesters as a means of generating a furore around the film. Certainly, the X-rating awarded to *Snuff* had been at the request of Shackleton, who had chosen to forego the R-rating that his film had originally been awarded suggesting that 'young people might be damaged by seeing explicit violence' (Eder, 1976). The only thing that stood to be damaged were his profits, should the film have been awarded an R-rating – this would have completely undermined the idea that *Snuff* was the 'bloodiest thing to ever happen in front of a camera' and derailed a marketing campaign that relied on constructing the film as 'the ultimate obscenity'. In New York, following limited interest in Indianapolis, Wichita and Las Vegas, the film became a *cause célèbre*, netting $59,512 in its first six days, and by March 10, a little over a month into its run, it had taken $157,062. The film's reputation was growing, and Shackleton had proved himself a canny entrepreneur, and with a lucrative idea, he had created a runaway hit.

The protestors increased in number when Shackleton's plants were joined by grass-roots feminist groups horrified by what the film promised. Perhaps one of the greatest legacies of the film is that it became the catalyst that would lead to the formation of the group Women Against Pornography (WAP, subsequently Women Against Violence Against Women – WAVAW), a mobilising force in the radical feminist movement. The group was led by Andrea Dworkin, a long-time activist who convinced her friends and mentors to join her in the picketing of the theatre in a nightly vigil (Brownmiller, 1999: 292). Less well known is that Dworkin found an unlikely (and probably unwanted) ally in the shape of the adult film industry, who also picketed the film feeling that it was doing irreparable damage to the reputation of their businesses. Veteran pornographic producer David F. Friedman recalls, that even before the production of *Snuff*:

> In the 1970s, a guy who was head of Campaign for Decency in Literature (which became the Campaign for Decency Through the Law – CDL) was making one of his

regular speeches on pornography when he suddenly came up with the allegation that the X-rated industry was torturing and killing performers on camera. (Friedman cited in Hebditch and Anning, 1988)

Hebditch and Anning detail that the Adult Film Association of America issued a statement to disassociate itself from the idea of the snuff movie and it appeared to go away, for a while at least. That was until Shackleton began developing a film with the intention of explicitly capitalising on the myth. It would, coincidentally, be David F. Friedman who Shackleton would approach for support when he began developing his new project; but Friedman refused, conscious of the irreparable damage that a film like that could do to his business. While Dworkin's Women Against Violence Against Women group were picketing screenings in New York, on the west coast a revivalist church group were picketing the film at Mann's Chinese Theater on Hollywood Boulevard, and in what is perhaps the ultimate irony of all of this, they stood side by side with Friedman and the Adult Association of America – the church group protesting what they saw as the ultimate pornography, and the Adult Association of America protesting what they saw as a corruption and misuse of the X-certificate, a category that they argued should be reserved solely for erotic material and not tarnished by association with a film like *Snuff* (Kaminsky, 1977: 9). It is notable that, even at this early point in the campaign, WAVAW were already conceding that while *Snuff* the film was a problem, it was simply a 'staged version of the underground snuff movies' (see figure 3). Nevertheless, Shackleton found himself at a curious intersection between anti-pornography feminists and anti-violence pornographers, with the film targeted by The League of New York Theatres and Producers as the most visible part of the growing pornography 'problem' on Times Square.

Nevertheless, the film was a runaway success. Indeed, Shackleton had been so confident that the film would be a success that even before its release he had already begun touting the sequel, *The Slasher.* In the same article in which Shackleton was promoting *Revenge of Cheerleaders* and *Fantastic Invasion of Planet Earth*, he spoke of the favourable response that the advertising campaign had received and suggested that a sequel would not be far behind (Cocchi, 1976). In April of 1977, and just as the initial furore that surrounded the release of *Snuff* was beginning to wane, Shackleton paired *Snuff* with *The Slasher* and enjoyed another successful run as a double bill. Much like the conclusion to

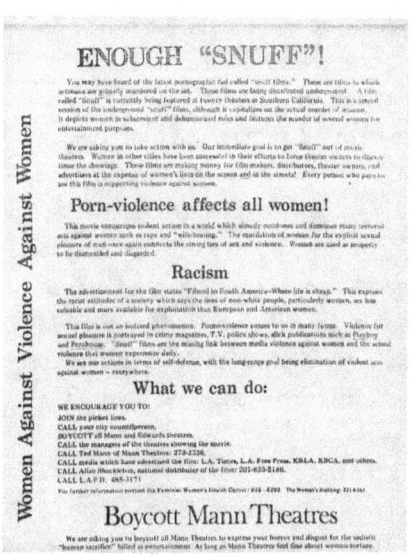

Fig. 3

Snuff itself, *The Slasher* was in no way related to *The Slaughter*, despite being pitched as a direct sequel (Variety, 1977: 20). The film was an Italian import that had previously been known as *Penetration, So Sweet, So Dead, The Slasher is a Sex Maniac* and finally, simply *The Slasher*. Significantly, the term 'slasher' was being used interchangeably in the press and feminist media as a synonym for the snuff movie, and while, as Richard Nowell has argued, the term slasher would later be applied to a variety of films without regard to content or form, the etymology of the nomenclature itself can be traced to press discourse that propagated concern about the existence of the snuff movie (2011: 17). Interestingly, despite the success of *Snuff* and Shackleton's suggestion that the film marked the beginning of a new period for Monarch in its shift away from pornography, *The Slasher* featured hard-core inserts starring Harry Reems.

DEBUNKING *SNUFF*

Even before the film's release, the industry papers had already debunked *Snuff*. Both *Boxoffice* and *Variety* had been sceptical from the start and were quick to disprove the claims of 'real murder', the latter tracking down Michael Findlay as the ultimate arbiter. During its initial run at New York's National Theater in Times Square, *New York Times* journalist Richard Eder shrewdly suggested that 'everything about the film is suspect: the contents, the promotion and possibly even some of the protest that is conducted each evening outside the box office' (1976: 13). However, the publicity and the protests made the film difficult to ignore, eventually prompting a series of complaints and then a petition to Manhattan's District Attorney, Robert M. Morgenthau. In turn, the petition attracted writers and legislators, including WAVAW organiser, Susan Brownmiller, the film critic, academic, and playwright, Eric Bentley and the Democrat Representative for Brooklyn Elizabeth Holtzman (1976: 13). They appealed to the D.A. to bring a criminal prosecution against Shackleton, but, after a month-long trial, Morgenthau determined that the film was 'nothing more than conventional trick photography' and that this was 'evident to anyone who sees the movie' (1976: 13). When Shackleton was challenged over the authenticity of the film, he conceded that if the film did indeed depict a real murder, he 'would be in jail in two minutes', but he also countered that with the suggestion that if it wasn't real, he would 'be a damn fool to admit it' too (*Variety*, 1976). Shackleton's refusal to own up to the construction didn't matter when Morgenthau eventually found the actress who had portrayed the victim, proving irrefutably that nobody had died on camera. *Boxoffice* magazine reported that the 'actress was embarrassed by her performance but certainly was not dismembered' and that as an aspiring actress she wanted to make a name for herself, just not in a film like *Snuff* (Anon, 1976a: ME-4). With this revelation, one might have expected the furore to subside. However, despite being faced with incontrovertible evidence, the idea refused to die, and the myth of snuff continued to grow.

Five years after the film's release, Andrea Dworkin remained steadfastly committed to her belief in the existence of snuff movies, and in her 1981 book, *Pornography: Men Possessing Women*, she maintained that 'in 1975 in the United States, organized crime reportedly sold "snuff" films to private collectors of pornography. In these films, women actually were maimed, sliced into pieces, fucked, and killed', and that crucially, these 'crimes were photographed and tape-recorded by the murderer, who played them back for pleasure' (1981: 71). Despite Dworkin's insistence, these were the same unsubstantiated rumours that had first inspired Shackleton to capitalise upon the snuff myth, and likely the same stories that originated with the Campaign for Decency in Literature.

Fig. 4

Nevertheless, Dworkin never faltered in her belief that women were being killed on camera, and although demonstrably unfounded, the snuff movie has remained a cinematic spectre that has haunted successive generations. In her book, *Battling Pornography: The American Feminist Anti-Pornography Movement 1976-1986* (2011), Carolyn Bronstein prints the last stanza of a previously unpublished poem in which the author, prominent feminist campaigner, Catherine Risingflame Moirai, details her initial responses to the film *Snuff*, and what she felt was an uncontrolled epidemic of 'snuff movies'.

> I am afraid
> when the woman on the screen
> was slit
> from throat to cunt
> when they pulled out her guts
> the men in the theatre stood yelling
> give me a knife
> give me a knife
> and then I went

> home
> I am afraid
> we are at war

Declaration of Catherine Risingflame Moirai (Printed in Bronstein, 2011: 85)

The poem is understandably emotive and honestly expresses the author's concerns over what she believed was happening in society, but what the poem demonstrates more than anything else is the power of an idea. The description of 'the woman on the screen' being 'slit from throat to cunt', is a hyperbolic misrepresentation of what actually happens in the film *Snuff*, and there are similarly misrepresentations in Bronstein's own account, in which she suggests that the killer chops off her fingers and toes and saws off her hands and her legs. As already detailed, aside from one finger and one hand, the rest of the 'victim' remains intact. These reports are demonstrably inaccurate, but nevertheless, feminist campaign groups like WAVAW quickly latched onto the film as a focal point through which they could articulate their concern, and it is in this way that the idea reverberated through society. By the time rumours of the snuff movie entered the UK, the British faction of WAVAW was suggesting that:

> pornography … ranges from page 3 in the *Sun*, through to *Penthouse*, *Les Girls*, and finally terminates in the horror of *Snuff* movies. Each magazine and booklet is full of images of women that are objectified, fetishized, violated, dehumanised and always degraded …. *Snuff* movies are films where women are actually killed as the climax in the pornographers' 'sick plot'. Cases have been discovered in California. (cited in Thompson, 1994: 90)

It is not without significance that the British version of the narrative imagined snuff as originating in California, where 'the Manson Family' murders had taken place. However, none of these accounts provide any evidence of the existence of snuff and simply continue to reprint rumours as evidence.

In the years since the film's original release, many have come forward to challenge the claims made about *Snuff* and, as already detailed, Julian Petley presents what is arguably the most convincing dismissal in his observation that the 'murder' is constructed according to Classical Hollywood styling. The sequence is comprised of multiple viewpoints that are edited together and assembled and this construction disrupts any sense that what we are being presented with is real (2000: 206). Similarly, the audio that is heard in the final moments of the sequence continues recording long after the film has run out, meaning that this audio would have needed to have been recorded externally and then post-synchronised to the visual track. While this practice is not unheard of (and was, for a long time, the principal means of production in Italy), the idea that in this instance the soundtrack was recorded separately and post-synchronised is preposterous. We are meant to believe that these are the last frames of footage caught by a single camera at the exact moment that the woman died. We hear the voices of the actors talking long after the visuals have ended, and, as a narrative device, it is incredibly effective. Unfortunately, it also demonstrates irrefutably that the sequence is staged and constructed. These issues when combined with the poor performances and shoddy special effects disrupt any sense of the film's authenticity and prove unequivocally that this is a cinematic construction that employs the coded conventions of the fiction film.

This is a perspective that was gradually accepted by some and one of the original protest organisers, writer and WAVAW member, Susan Brownmiller, would later acknowledge that while the rumours of real murder had been greatly exaggerated to the degree that they had evaporated under investigation, the film's themes of eroticized torture had galvanised the feminist movement against pornography in the 1970s (Brownmiller, 1999: 292). This concession can be seen in the copy from the leaflets that were distributed at the protest in New York, that state:

> We are opposed to the filming, distribution and mass-marketing of the film "snuff" ... Whether or not the death depicted in the current film "Snuff" is real or simulated is not the issue. That sexual violence is presented as entertainment, that the murder and dismemberment of a woman's body is commercial film material is an outrage to our sense of justice as women, as human beings. We – and all are welcome to join our efforts – will leaflet, picket, write letters, to do what is necessary to prevent the showing of the film "Snuff" in New York City. We can not allow murder for profit.
> (reprinted in Lyons 1997: 65)

This shift was documented by Linda Williams, who detailed how for many anti-pornography feminists the source of the horror simply 'shifted from the sadistic content of the film to the sadism of viewers who would pay to see what they thought was the ultimate orgasm' (1989: 42). Williams describes this as a kind of 'generic confusion' in which the culmination of hard-core pornography could now include images of death and the involuntary death-spasm. While the imagery within *Snuff* was demonstrably staged, it was widely believed that it reflected the apotheosis of male desire and, perhaps most importantly, had the potential to incite sexualised violence against women. Eithne Johnson and Eric Schaefer have argued that this shift in discourse was strategically deployed, as a means of shifting 'the definition of pornography – from sexual representation to a literal inscription of male dominance over woman' (1993: 56). When faced with a lack of verifiable evidence, the willingness of an audience of men to watch imagery like this became evidence enough of their desire for eroticised murder and this, perhaps more than anything else, allowed the myth of snuff to persist and evolve.

This is how the idea of snuff grew, and in spite of the many ways in which the film failed to construct a convincing conclusion to its narrative, it is its central idea that has remained the most important aspect of its success. The film itself has been described as 'a stilted and amateurish exploitation quickie [that] purported to be an actual snuff film' (Groves, n.d.). Another commentator credited the film with the dubious honour of 'the worst scripted, most incompetently made, and horrendously dubbed movies [that they had] EVER seen' (Tingle, 2012, emphasis in original). However, and irrespective of its many technical failures, its central conceit, that someone was killed on camera for financial gain and the sexual gratification of others has continued to resonate and has ensured that the myth of the snuff movie survives. Periodically, rumours of the emergence of the snuff movie will resurface, just as they had in New York, and as I will demonstrate in later chapters, the descriptions often appear to be referencing Shackleton's film *Snuff* rather than an actual snuff movie. Much like John Ford's *The Man Who Shot Liberty Valance* (1962), rather than scrutinise the story that they are retelling, reporters have chosen to recount a fiction because its sensationalist narrative will continue to sell newspapers. The chapter that follows traces the cultural and industrial origins of the film, exploring the link to 'the Manson Family' and to the Tate/LaBianca murders, before considering the industrial contexts that gave rise to the film in the first place, charting how through a series of Supreme Court rulings, *Snuff* became the obvious evolution to a genre that was already blending themes of sex and violence..

Chapter 2. The Origins of *Snuff*

Although the decision to shoot the now infamous ending to *Snuff* came from Allan Shackleton and not from Michael and Roberta Findlay, in many ways, Shackleton's coda represents the natural conclusion to the career of a couple whose work together had always blended acts of sex and violence. From their earliest collaboration in 1964 with *Body of a Female*, a film in which a stripper is abducted by a drifter and delivered into bondage to be tortured by a wealthy pervert, through to their breakthrough film in 1967, *The Touch of Her Flesh*, and the film's subsequent sequels *The Curse of Her Flesh* and *The Kiss of Her Flesh* (both 1968), the Findlays' work frequently returned to explore themes of sexual violence, themes that can be seen to reach their violent, if unconvincing conclusion in Shackleton's *Snuff* coda.

Fig. 5

So aligned were they to this aesthetic that their earlier work contributes to a discrete subset of the exploitation film commonly known as the 'roughies'. The 'roughies' are an aggressive strain of sexploitation cinema that applied violence and sadism to the already established 'nudie cutie' formula. These films routinely featured stories that involved women being sold into slavery, becoming hooked on drugs, and, in their hardcore iterations, invariably concluded with them being forced to have rough sex with their kidnappers. An emphasis on bondage, sadomasochism and rough and violent sexual abuse giving name to the aggressive sub-genre. Producers of the genre exploited a series of United States Supreme Court rulings throughout the 1950s and the 1960s that had led to successive relaxations in the laws governing what was permissible, and in doing so, helped to redefine what was considered obscene in the eyes of the law (Freedman and D'Emilio, 2012: 286). In film, this relaxation is typically seen to culminate in the 'Golden Age of Pornography', or what Ralph Blumenthal of *The New York Times* called 'Porno Chic' (1973: 28). Throughout this period, for a short time at least, pornography became accepted as part of mainstream entertainment. The success of the genre is often attributed to the popularity of *Deep Throat* in 1972, a film which reportedly saw celebrities, diplomats, critics, businessmen, dating couples, and even lone women attend the sold-out screenings of a film that was described as 'the *Ben-Hur* of porno pix' (Blumenthal, 1973: 28). Blumenthal details how the film had 'become a premier topic of cocktail-party and dinner-table conversation in Manhattan drawing rooms, Long Island beach cottages and ski country A-frames' (1973: 28). However, for all of the genre's popularity and apparent acceptability, the visibility of pornography would be short-lived, and by 1975 a conservative backlash was already being felt, with *Snuff* the focal point for much of this attention. While not pornographic, *Snuff*, much like the 'roughies' that had preceded it, presented its murderous conclusion as a sexually motivated attack, and because of this, the film would become a mobilising force in the battle against pornography.

While the aim of the previous chapter was to introduce the film *Snuff*, and explore the ways that it both capitalised on, and furthered the belief in the myth of the snuff movie, the aim of this chapter is to consider the cultural and industrial contexts that gave rise to *Snuff* in the first place.

THE CULTURAL ORIGINS OF THE SNUFF MOVIE

Almost all works that consider the myth of the snuff movie take Ed Sanders' book-length expose of 'the Manson Family' (1972) as a starting point, and while most seek to challenge that narrative that he presents, the sum effect of this repetition has irrevocably linked the urban legend to the Manson Family murders (see Jackson, 2003; Jones and Carlin, 2016; Kerekes and Slater, 1994). Much of the association is circumstantial and is based on the knowledge that 'the Family' routinely filmed their day-to-day lives with three Super 8mm cameras and were even rumoured to have stolen a 35mm production quality movie camera from an NBC television network van. When Sanders interviewed family member Vern Plumlee about the nature of the films that the family produced, Plumlee claimed that it was 'just goofy things', the effects of an acid trip, 'The Family' dancing around with knives, or more commonly, pornography, occasionally with famous participants (Sanders, 1972: 185).

This emphasis on pornography is mirrored in another account detailed by Sanders, in which a source who was posing as a New York pornography dealer, handling outtakes of Andy Warhol films (presumably from *Blue Movie* [1969]) was allegedly given the opportunity to purchase seven hours of pornography that had been produced by 'the Family' but claimed that the $250,000 price tag proved too difficult to justify (1972: 186). Significantly, Sanders' account conflates the reports of the circulation of 'Family' produced pornography, with another report that claimed that films of the 'Malibu and San Francisco Ax [sic] murders' were also believed to be circulating illegally via similar networks. Sanders' source even claimed that 'the Family' had produced so many films that they had even begun to categorise them into rudimentary genres. The first, corroborating Vern Plumlee's account, were films of the 'Family dancing and loving', giving credence to the rumours of the existence of pornographic films that featured 'the Family'; the second were films of animal sacrifice, which Sanders' book suggests often resulted in orgies in which 'Family' members drank the blood of cats and dogs before smearing it upon their bodies and having sex in the desert; and the third, which would forever tie both 'the Manson Family' and Sanders to the myth of the snuff movie, was the suggestion that he had seen films of 'the Family' engaged in ritualistic human sacrifice (1972: 186). Sanders reprints a transcript of an interview in his book, but when pressed on the details, Sanders' source was vague and non-committal. In places Sanders is clearly leading the interviewee, and as a result, it is not the most reliable source of information. For instance, when asked on what day of the week the gang met at a private beach in Malibu, his source replies 'Wednesday'. Sanders then asks if they met on a full moon, presumably hoping to capitalise on the rumours of a satanic ritual, to which the respondent replies unconvincingly, 'or full moon, whatever', 'something like that' (1972: 189). When Sanders asks him directly about rumours of 'snuff movies' the respondent is similarly vague but describes a home movie that documented a satanic ritual in which the participants wore black hoods around the already dead body of a naked and decapitated girl. When Sanders asks, 'what was the rest of the movie like?', he replies 'I didn't see it. I just, you know?' (1972: 190). Sanders doesn't press him on the details but his response was presumably going to be that he didn't see it, and that he had only heard about it. Nevertheless, and despite the unreliability of this evidence, Sanders uses it as proof of 'the Family's' link to snuff movies, suggesting that Manson produced 'torrid video-porn' and 'brutality-films' (the name that Sanders gives to snuff movies) in Death Valley in the Summer of 1969 (1972: 164). This is widely acknowledged as the first recorded use of the term, and although Sanders never explicitly links the idea of the snuff movie to the Tate/LaBianca murders, as the first reports began to emerge about the grisly murder of the twenty-six-year-old fashion model and film star Sharon Tate, inevitably, speculation began to build that 'the Family' had captured her brutal murder on camera. Indeed, so tied are 'the Manson Family' to the myth of the snuff movie that the early reports of snuff movies entering New York from South America even attribute the term 'snuff movie' to Manson himself, a perspective that was no doubt exacerbated by the circulation of the horrific crime scene photographs (Anon, 1975d). While Sanders' account works hard to try and connect 'the Manson Family' to the idea of the snuff movie, they would become irrevocably linked through the production of *Snuff*, a film that emerges from the convergence and expansion of the art and exploitation markets.

REAL MURDER AND THE DEATH OF PORNO CHIC

Eithne Johnson and Eric Schaefer have suggested that '*Snuff* stands as the pivotal moment in a discursive shift in debates about pornography and sexual representation'. They argue that 'before *Snuff*, pornography had been viewed generally as a victimless vice or more controversially as an expression of sexual liberation', but that after its release, attitudes can be seen to swing back towards a far more conservative stance that sees pornography '(re)stigmatized as a dangerous form of low culture that legitimized the exploitation of women and children for a sadistic, presumably male audience' (1993: 40). However, as tempting as it is to construct a clear narrative of cause and effect and attribute the backlash against pornography simply to the release of *Snuff*, if Shackleton is to be believed then this backlash began much earlier, and the production of *Snuff* was, at least in part, inspired as a response to these shifting sensibilities and the increasingly hostile climate towards pornography. While *Snuff* unquestionably became a focal point and a mobilising force for a number of different feminist groups, we need to be careful about constructing a narrative in which *Snuff* presents something foreign or new to the American film market. One of the real dangers of such neat narratives is that they imagine *Snuff* as an anomaly, without historical precedent, and in doing so, ignore the long tradition of filmmaking on which *Snuff* was drawing.

In his analysis of the snuff myth, Boaz Hagin argues that the standard history of the evolution of the snuff movie is incomplete and that by considering the relationship of snuff to popular Hollywood films 'a different historical account can be constructed' (2010: 44). Hagin makes links to examples of films from the Classical era in which characters, often journalists, actively interfere with cases in ways that cause, or come close to causing, real death, citing the 'sensation-seeking, if not bloodthirsty, public [that] is assumed to exist in these and many other Hollywood films' (2010: 44). Hagin links these conceptually to the idea of snuff and suggests that this work gives an indication of what kinds of historiographical work remains to be done to chart the emergence of the snuff myth in film. While his analysis is completely focused upon the text, it does suggest that there are other ways to conceive of this history.

For the remainder of this chapter, rather than consider *Snuff* as an anomaly in the development of American exploitation cinema, I will locate *Snuff* within a longer tradition of popular American film and consider it as a point of convergence for a number of broader cinematic trends that were increasingly visible across the art-house and exploitation circuits. I will explore how these trends were facilitated by a series of landmark Supreme Court rulings that ushered in a period of greater liberalisation and that ultimately led to the erosion of the Motion Picture Production Code and, with that, a greater emphasis on narratives that prioritised sex and violence, culminating in *Snuff*.

In 1948, the Supreme Court of the United States of America approved a landmark ruling that would dramatically alter the trajectory of the popular film. United States v. Paramount Pictures, Inc., more popularly as the 'Paramount Decree', ruled it unlawful for the Hollywood studios to own their own theatres, and with that, the system of vertical integration that had reinforced their dominance of the industry collapsed. Up until 1948, the major Hollywood studios controlled the means of production, distribution, and exhibition, creating an oligopoly that suppressed competition. The studios held the writers, directors, producers and actors under contract, their studios produced and processed the films, and they owned a small number of theatres in which their films were then exhibited. However, because these theatres were the biggest and most centrally located, they generated the most profits, leaving little room for the independent sector to operate on the fringes of the industry. However, when the Supreme Court found the majors guilty of oligopolistic practice and ordered them to sell off their theatre chains, they were then forced to compete on a more democratic basis. The result of this was that the studio system of production that had benefited the major distributors since the late 1910s began to collapse, resulting in a dramatic decline in the number of films being produced every year (see Tzioumakis, 2006: 101).

An unforeseen effect of this democratisation would be the weakening of the Motion Picture Production Code – a set of moral guidelines around the production of film that had governed the industry since 1934. Early iterations of what would eventually become the Code were established in 1924 in response to a series of high-profile scandals that had seriously damaged Hollywood's public image. The murder of William Desmond Taylor (a leading film director of the silent era) in February 1922 sent shockwaves through Hollywood, coming only a year after celebrated comedian Roscoe 'Fatty' Arbuckle, was accused of the rape and murder of model and actress Virginia Rappe in September 1921. These scandals led to political pressure to clean up the industry and the development of guidelines that dictated what would be deemed acceptable on screen from that point on. The Motion Pictures and Distributors Association of America made initial attempts to govern the industry through a formula, and then in 1926, through a system that prescriptively grouped content into 'Don'ts' – subject matter that should never appear in a motion picture under any circumstance – and 'Be Carefuls' – material that, if it did appear, should be handled with the utmost sensitivity.

These conservative guidelines would become the precursor of the Motion Picture

Production Code, which was introduced in 1934 and governed the production of mainstream Hollywood film until 1968. Preventing the studios from owning theatre chains benefited the independent theatres, who, no longer tied to exhibiting Hollywood's product and in need of content of their own, began showing foreign and independently produced films that were created by producers who were not members of Motion Picture Producers and Distributors of America (MPPDA).[1] Because of this, these films often took a more liberal approach to the depiction of sex and violence, and the inconsistency in the way that content was regulated would help to reshape the market for popular film.[2]

The reason that the Code did not affect imported or independently produced film was that it was ostensibly a voluntary scheme that was not enshrined in law. It had been developed in conjunction with the studios as a way of staving off the growing pressure from groups such as the Catholic Legion of Decency, and because of that, it functioned more like a gentlemen's agreement between the studios and the theatres to self-censor based upon a prescribed list of morally acceptable representations. The voluntary nature of this system benefitted the independent sector enormously by allowing them to import and produce content that would never be allowed under the confines of the Code. However, that did not mean that they went without scrutiny. Alongside State Review and censorship boards, a variety of regulations relating to obscenity governed mainstream Hollywood production and independent production alike, but it was only through the continual pushing of these boundaries that the independents were able to begin reshaping the film industry, eventually leading to the collapse of the Code.

The first such instance happened in 1952 when film distributor Joseph Burstyn appealed to the Supreme Court after the state of New York withdrew his license to exhibit the short film *The Miracle* (1952). *The Miracle* was part of Italian neorealist Roberto Rossellini's film *L'Amore* (1948), and whereas in Italy the film had been celebrated, with actress Anna Magnani winning the Nastro d'Argento (Silver Ribbon) in 1949 for best actress for her performance in the film, in New York, the film triggered a furore, with many labelling it blasphemous. Edward T. McCaffrey, the Commissioner for Licenses, found the film 'officially and personally blasphemous' and illegally over-rode the Board's decision to release the film when he revoked its license (Randall, 1968: 28). McCaffrey was a prominent Catholic and sought support from the Catholic Legion of Decency in the condemnation of the film. In 1950, the influence of the Church in Hollywood was nearly absolute, but they held little sway over the content of imported films (see Wittern-Keller and Haberski, Jr., 2008), and it was this loophole that allowed Burstyn to challenge the ruling. Officers at a local office or bureau could refuse a licence if a film was considered to be obscene, indecent, immoral, inhuman or sacrilegious. The licence for *The Miracle* had been repealed on this basis, but Burstyn challenged the ruling arguing that the statute contravened his First Amendment rights. In May 1952 and after a lengthy debate, the Supreme Court agreed, ruling that the term 'sacrilegious' was not permissible under law and that Burstyn's right to free speech should be upheld under the First Amendment guarantees. This was an important case, and overturned a 1915 ruling that held that since film was a business, it did not warrant protection under the First Amendment laws. American Civil Liberties Union historian Samuel Walker has argued that *The Miracle* ruling was 'the beginning of the end of film censorship' in the United States (1999: 231), opening the door for further challenges around the regulation of film.

The following year, the Court of Appeal heard the case of Commercial Pictures Corp. v. Board of Regents of University State of New York. Commercial Pictures was appealing the decision to refuse a licence to exhibit the French film *La Ronde* (1950) on the grounds that it was 'immoral' and 'would tend to corrupt morals'. Commercial Pictures challenged the decision to deny the film a license, arguing that:

(1) Censorship of film was unconstitutional.

(2) Even if licensing or censorship were permissible, the statutory standards for denying a license on the grounds that a film is 'immoral' and 'would tend to corrupt morals' was unconstitutionally vague and indefinite.

(3) Even if the standards were not unconstitutional, they were improperly applied to *La Ronde*. (Meyer et al., 2006: 241)

The Supreme Court drew upon the precedent of the *Miracle* decision, and although contentious, eventually ruled that the ambiguity of terms like 'sacrilegious', and the perception of what may constitute morality or immorality, were 'unconstitutionally vague as standards for licensing motion pictures'. They instead insisted that a workable definition of immorality should be added to the statute books to assist in future cases when judging what may and may not be considered obscene (Meyer et al., 2006: 246). From this, the Supreme Court ruled that a motion picture could be deemed to be immoral if it portrayed 'acts of sexual immorality … as desirable, acceptable, or proper patterns of behaviour' (Matter of Excelsior Pict. Corp. v. Regents, 1957), a definition that would soon be tested with the release of *Garden of Eden* (1954).

In 1957, Excelsior Pictures challenged the New York Board of Regents over its belief that *Garden of Eden* was indecent, immoral and therefore obscene. The basis for the claim was that the film was set in a nudist colony and presented a thinly veiled plot that allowed the producers to show nudists playing volleyball, sunbathing and water-skiing (see Lewis, 2000: 200). The film did not show full-frontal nudity – when full figures were in view, both men and women were shown from behind. When the New York State Court of Appeals found in favour of Excelsior Pictures and ruled that onscreen nudity was not obscene, this opened the door to a new wave of exploitation cinema with producers who were only too keen to capitalise on the potential for titillation that this ruling offered.

One of the first films to openly exploit the ruling was Russ Meyer's independently produced debut feature, *The Immoral Mr Teas* (1959). The film follows the adventures of a door-to-door salesman and his interactions with beautiful, buxom women. Subtle, it was not, and although a precedent for on-screen nudity had already been set with *Garden of Eden*, *The Immoral Mr Teas* was more direct, going as far as to sexualise the women that Mr Teas followed around. Because of that, the film did not pass without scrutiny, and Edward Seretsky, the owner of Aabbe Art Cinema in Philadelphia was arrested for screening the film. However, he was later released after a jury acquitted the film and the presiding judge ruled it 'vulgar, pointless' and 'in bad taste … but not pornography' (*Variety*, 1960: 7). Hailed as the first of the 'nudie-cuties' – suggestive comedies that featured nudity but generally no touching – Meyer's film would inspire a wave of newly minted genres, with distributors keen to capitalise on the shifting sensibilities around nudity on screen.

It is a cycle of films that follows the 'nudie-cuties' to which *Snuff* is most indebted. In 1963, sensing that the success of the anodyne 'nudie-cutie' format was beginning to wane, but also bitterly aware that the merest glimpse of pubic hair would attract the ire of the authorities, producer David F. Friedman and director Herschell Gordon Lewis injected the threat of sexual violence into the mix with *Scum of the Earth!* (1963). *Scum of the Earth!*, though mild in its presentation, is credited as the first 'roughie', and significantly, like *Snuff* itself, employs a narrative in which pornographers exploit the vulnerability of a lone female subject on camera. While the film does not result in the murder of the protagonist, it can certainly be seen as a precursor to Shackleton's *Snuff*, and inspired more production in this area. The popularity of these films led to increasingly exploitative fair. First came the 'kinkies'; films that revelled in the depiction of fetishist sexual practice, a sub-genre that included films like Ed Wood's *White Slaves of Chinatown* (1964), Joseph Mawra's *Olga's House of Shame* (1964), and the would-be 'video nasty' *Love Camp 7* (1969). Lewis and Friedman would also go on to create the 'ghoulie' with what is universally regarded as the first gore film, *Blood Feast* in 1963, another film that would later find notoriety on the Department of Public Prosecutions 'video nasties' list in the UK. The 'roughies' genre developed further when George Weiss, the producer of *White Slaves of Chinatown* and Mawra's *Olga* series approached the Findlays to direct something in the genre and they developed the aforementioned *Body of a Female*, and the lesser-seen *Satan's Bed* (1965), starring a then-unknown Yoko Ono. The popularity of these films would lead to the Findlays' greatest success, *The Touch of Her Flesh* in 1967, and *The Curse of her Flesh* and *The Kiss of Her Flesh*, both 1968, and all films that successfully blended of sex and violence in a way not previously seen.

When the Code was eventually abolished in 1968, it made it easier to produce risqué content, but that does not mean there were not periodic backlashes. In 1969, Andy Warhol's hardcore feature film *Blue Movie* (also known as *Fuck*) was seized by the police under obscenity laws less than a month after it had opened. Warhol retaliated by publishing the film as a book, but its release nevertheless signalled a shift that would see pornography move from the fringes of the grindhouse to the front page of the *New York Times*, with Ralph Blumenthal's influential article on the new 'porno chic'. This relaxation inspired many producers to move into the production of hardcore pornography (the Findlays included); but many did so by still blending representations of sex and violence, and one of the more interesting films to come out of this tradition, particularly in relation to *Snuff*, is Sidney Knight's *The Debauchers* from 1970. The film is significant because it concludes with a snuff-style coda in which the protagonist, played by Tina Russell, manages to overpower and kill her co-star who intended to murder her on camera at the behest of the director. The director is ultimately placated since he still has a murder in the film. Were the narrative trajectory not significant enough, this film is made all the more significant because Sidney Knight was, in fact, a pseudonym used by Simon Nuchtern, the director that Carter Stevens would hire to complete Shackleton's vision for *Snuff* some six years later, no doubt inspired by the conclusion to *The Debauchers*.

The 1970s continued to see a relaxation in attitudes surrounding pornography. The commercialisation of *Deep Throat*, *Behind the Green Door* (1972), *The Devil in Miss Jones* in 1973, and *The Opening of Misty Beethoven* in 1976, the same year that *Snuff* was released, all worked to popularise the genre. However, these were not the hardcore stag loops of old; many of these films sought to elevate the genre. *The Devil in Miss Jones* was inspired by Jean-Paul Sartre's existentialist 1944 play *No Exit*, while *The Opening of Misty Beethoven* reworked George Bernard Shaw's *Pygmalion*, the basis for *My Fair Lady* (1964). While these films presented the acceptable face of hardcore pornography, *The Debauchers*, and the strain of 'roughie' inspired pornography that it belongs to, were something entirely different. Although the cycle would be short-lived, it would give rise to some of the most challenging commercially available pornography ever produced – films like *Forced Entry* (1973), in which a psychotic Vietnam veteran sexually assaults and kills women, or *Water Power* (1976), a film loosely based upon the real-life case of Michael Hubert Kenyon, known as the 'enema-bandit', a rapist who would perform enemas on his victims. Neil Jackson has observed that the hardcore evolution of the roughie cycle that was facilitated by films like *Forced Entry* consolidates 'the generic fusion of realist horror and sex film conventions, often focusing upon the activities of lone sexual sadists', such as the 'serial sex murderers such as Albert DeSalvo, Ted Bundy, and Kenneth Bianchi/Angelo Buono' (2017: 299). Although *Snuff* does not belong to this subset of hardcore pornography, it is the same impulse to consolidate sex and violence that informs the production of *Snuff*. *Snuff* offers the same emphasis on sexualised violence and reworks the image of a recognisable contemporary serial killer, Charles Manson, in a fictional context. But crucially, *Snuff* is neither hardcore pornography, nor is it a convincing representation of violence. However, what it proved to be was an incredibly useful, visible and viable conduit for groups wanting to protest against the treatment and representation of women in pornography. Therefore, it is important to acknowledge that despite Johnson and Schaefer's suggestion that '*Snuff* stands as the pivotal moment in a discursive shift in debates about pornography and sexual representation' (1993: 40), this is not because *Snuff* stood out as particularly excessive, or even because it stood as an anomaly. As we have already seen, there was a variety of films throughout this period that offered similar narratives (and which were often far more extreme in their presentation, dating back to Nuchtern's *The Debauchers*). What *Snuff* did do was provide a focus for radical feminist groups who were keen to fight back against what they felt were misogynistic representations and treatment of women in film, evident in a genre that can be seen to begin some thirteen years earlier with *Scum of the Earth!*

FOOTNOTES

1. In 1945 the MPPDA became the MPAA, the Motion Picture Association of America.
2. Significantly, MPAA members – the studios – often released risqué films through subsidiaries (Lopert for United Artists, and Kingsleigh for Columbia).

Chapter 3. The Authenticity of *Snuff*

While *Snuff* presented an array of problems for the distributors domestically in the United States, it never received a theatrical release in the United Kingdom. It would be six years before the film would finally find its way to the British market and when it did, the film found itself at the centre of another controversy. A conservative backlash against the burgeoning video industry was already being felt and by the early part of 1982, when *Snuff* was scheduled for release, this was in full swing. The press were speculating about the threat that horror videos posed, particularly to children who figured centrally in *The Daily Mail*'s campaign to 'Ban the Sadist Videos' (Miles, 1983: 1-2). The claims of 'real murder' in relation to *Snuff* made it prime fodder for this kind of sensationalist tabloid coverage and as these stories began to reverberate through the press the distributor tried to distance itself from the release.

Snuff was always going to be a contentious film. It had been scheduled for release by Astra Video in 1982, but when the company found itself at the centre of a scandal, it claimed that, in light of the negative attention, it had taken the decision to not release the film and that the version that had come to market was a bootleg which had nothing at all to do with them. Astra Video's claim rested on the fact that the packaging for the available version was completely devoid of any reference to the company. The spine of the video sleeve didn't even list the film's title and the labels on the cassette had a distinctly amateurish feel to them. Since the Department of Public Prosecutions was unable to prove conclusively that the film was linked to Astra, the company narrowly avoided prosecution.

In the years since, a vibrant community has grown up around the 'video nasties' and the cassettes change hands for increasingly large sums of money. The rarest of these, Luigi Patella's *The Beast in Heat* (1977) is now worth close to £2000 but, as with any collectible, provenance and authenticity are of paramount importance. The muddy distribution history of *Snuff* has long left a question mark hanging over the legitimacy of the release and this issue has only been compounded by the fact that two versions exist: a black-sleeved variant that is by far the most common and is considered by many to be the authentic release; and a second version, a blue-sleeved variant that is contested by many collectors as an inauthentic bootleg created in the 1990s to capitalise on the booming trade in 'video nasties'.

This mystery has led to years of speculation about who released the film originally, and while in the wider public consciousness the debate surrounding *Snuff* relates explicitly to the authenticity of the murder (an allegation that can be quickly debunked by anyone who cares to watch the film), within the subculture of the British video collectors' market, a second debate persists about the legitimacy of either of the two releases. This chapter documents this history and explores the discourse that surrounds the release, assessing the ways in which the absence of an official, traceable history inadvertently contributed to the cultural mythology of the snuff movie in the UK and, perhaps, allowed the concept of the snuff movie to pass into the popular consciousness in a way that an official, traceable history may have prevented.

NASTY BUSINESS

The 'video nasties' furore is a curious and implausible moment in British history that culminates in the introduction of the Video Recordings Act, through which what was considered indecent, immoral, and obscene in the realm of the moving image was redrawn. In 1982, just as home video was finding a foothold in the UK, a moral panic erupted about the advertising that was being used to promote a rage of videocassettes that had been released to the British market. A journalist (Chippendale, 1982) dubbed the films the 'video nasties' and the name stuck, soon being used to describe a wide range of films irrespective of genre or content. This coverage attracted the attention of the Director of Public Prosecutions (DPP) who began raiding the premises of wholesalers, distributors and retailers found to be stocking the 'video nasties'. The problem for the industry was that the label was largely meaningless and while some, such as journalist Peter Chippendale, had attempted to define what they felt were the characteristics of a 'video nasty' – films released on video that revelled in 'murder, multiple rape, butchery, sado-masochism, mutilation of women, cannibalism and Nazi atrocities' (Chippendale, 1982) – the label itself was fluid and subject to interpretation. Without clear definition of what might constitute a 'video nasty', the video industry had little idea of what was likely to land them in court.

A test case was brought against the distributor VIPCO at Willesden Magistrates Court in London on August 31, 1982 in which the prosecution described the offending material as 'an extravaganza of gory violence, capable of depraving and corrupting those that watched'. The distributor was required to forfeit 590 copies of their cassettes (*The Driller Killer*, 1979, and *Death Trap*, 1976) plus the master tapes to prevent any further reproduction, with the presiding Judge quoted as saying that this should provide a 'clear warning' to other distributors, and that if the Department of Public Prosecutions was to seek prosecutions under Section 2 of the Obscene Publications Act, there was every likelihood of fines and/or imprisonment. A spate of prosecutions indeed began, with videocassettes routinely confiscated and destroyed in action that is typically seen to reach its improbable conclusion on 3 February 1984, with the imprisonment of David Hamilton Grant. Grant, director of the company World of Video 2000, was sentenced to six months in prison for releasing *Nightmares in a Damaged Brain*, (1981) in a version that was marginally longer than its theatrically certified counterpart.

Shortly afterwards, an Act of Parliament mandated that any commercial video recordings offered for sale or for hire within the UK must carry a classification been agreed upon by an authority designated by the Home Office, in this case, the British Board of Film Classification (BBFC). From that point on, it became an offense to supply a film on video without a certificate, and the films that had been released on video up until that point were required to go through the same certification process. Because of the costs associated with this, many distributors took the decision to not certificate their back catalogues, and instead withdrew these videos from circulation. This period before the industry was regulated has become known as 'pre-certification'; literally, films that were released on video before it was a requirement that they were certificated by the BBFC. There are obviously illicit connotations here and, in the years since, the appeal of a market that existed before regulation has become much mythologised (see McKenna, 2020; Walker, 2022). However, for the purposes of this chapter, it is important to understand that the video nasties, and 'pre-certs' more generally, are increasingly valuable and contribute to a vibrant market, with collectors deeply invested in preserving and archiving video culture from this period.

BLACK-SLEEVED *SNUFF*

In 1982, a newly formed distributor launched an aggressive advertising campaign to promote its new range of titles. Astra Video was a British company headed up by Mike Behr and backed by the Los Angeles-based distributor, Wizard Video (controlled by Charles Band). The company's earliest releases were a series of contentious Wizard titles, designed to grab the attention of the British video renting public. They released *The Best of Sex and Violence* (1982), a compilation of the most salacious clips from a range of exploitation titles that was hosted by John Carradine. The film was presented as assembling 'all the entertaining elements from forty of the most lurid features of the last decade [in] one exploitation extravaganza—the ultimate orgy and sex and violence'. Astra released Meir Zarchi's still-controversial rape/revenge film *I Spit on Your Grave* (1978), and Herschell Gordon Lewis' trail-blazing low budget gore film, and prototypical 'ghoulie', *Blood Feast*. The latter two, along with *Snuff*, would find their way on to the DPP's 'video nasty' list and would forever link Astra Video to the moral panic.

There was a growing climate of concern and a wave of anxiety around the threat that violent videos posed. However, Behr chose to ignore this, claiming that he wasn't worried about *Snuff* (or any other) release and suggested that since they were 'no censorship laws on video at all. What can they do about it?' (Chippendale, 1982). This was a question that would come back to haunt Behr as momentum against the 'video nasties' grew, and *Snuff* found itself at the centre of a campaign that sought to 'Ban the Sadist Videos'. *The Daily Express* singled the film out as a particularly problematic example of the pseudo-genre:

> A new commodity will be available in your high street next week—a film called "Snuff" which anyone will be able to buy over the counter at some of the 12,000 video shops throughout Britain. It shows scenes of rape and mutilation and murder so realistic that the cover asks: "are the killings in the film for real?" (Dawe, 1982)

Slowly recognising the potential backlash that he was facing, Behr made some attempts at damage limitation and tried to clarify his position in an interview with the trade magazine *Video Business*. He said 'of course it's not a real snuff movie … It's a publicity stunt' and claimed that he had always expected that '[the] release of the film would lead to problems', and because of the controversy they would only be keeping the film on the market for about a month (Anon, 1982a). Here he suggests that the company had already taken orders for 2500 units on the first day of release, a statement that is significant for two reasons: firstly, because it highlights that *Snuff* was only ever intended to be a limited release, with a recognition by Behr that the provocative nature of the film would likely land him in hot water; but secondly, and perhaps more importantly, because it suggests that the film was *already* available and was *already* a huge success (those 2500 units equating to around £100,000 in revenue).

Fig. 6

The same issue of *Video Business* carried a full-page advertisement for *Blood Feast* and *Snuff* in a style evocative of an American grindhouse double-bill. The promotional campaign titled 'Wall-to-Wall Gore' had been supplied to Astra by Charles Band via his company Wizard, and while the artwork for *Blood Feast* reworked a US theatrical release poster for its design, *Snuff* used a newly commissioned design that differed significantly from the US campaign. Where the American theatrical publicity campaign sported a do-it-yourself aesthetic more in keeping with the concept of *Snuff*, in the UK this aesthetic was replaced by a more traditional and polished design that suggested more routine horror fare than was promised by the taglines (see Fig. 6).

Nevertheless, the change of aesthetic did little to protect the film from attacks in the tabloid press; possibly feeling the pressure building, Behr printed a retraction in the next issue of *Video Business*. Here he stated that the company had no choice but to cancel this release, suggesting that Astra '[feel[s] that the publicity surrounding it will lead the buying public into purchasing a movie that has been sensationalised into something that it is not'. Astra was '[p]roud of its reputation for integrity and honesty', and did 'not want to cash-in on false publicity' (*Video Business*, 1982b: 4). However, Astra had already acknowledged that the release would be controversial, and in interviews leading up to its release seemed to welcome the publicity that controversy would bring, even actively courting that controversy with Behr's brash come-on of 'what can they do about it?'. The resulting media coverage would appear to be commensurate with that expectation, but the retraction suggests that Behr had finally realised the gravity of the situation and his suggestion that the movie 'ha[d] been sensationalised into something that it is not' (*Video Business*, 1982b: 4), illustrates a more cautious approach not evident in his earlier statements.

He was right to be cautious. The climate had changed significantly, and he found himself caught in the centre of a storm. On June 9, 1982, the Obscene Publications Squad conducted raids on premises of three video distributors; Go Video, VIPCO and Astra, confiscating VHS and Betamax copies of *SS Experiment Camp* (1976), *Driller Killer* and *I Spit on Your Grave* respectively. Almost in reply to Behr's taunt of 'what can they do about it?', the squad seized three hundred copies of *I Spit on Your Grave* from Astra Video's Croydon offices. These seizures would eventually lead to the first wave of prosecutions that focussed explicitly on distributors of video cassettes, rather than prosecuting rental shops or the general video renting public. This was a new strategy that sought to stem the problem of the 'video nasties' at its source.

In an interview for the book *Shock Horror: Astounding Artwork from the Video Nasty Era* (Brewster, Fenton and Morris, 2005), Behr claimed that following his problems with the authorities over the release of *I Spit on Your Grave*, he was advised by his solicitor that under no circumstances was he to attempt to distribute *Snuff*, and that, based upon this advice, he took the decision to withdraw the film from the market. However, this is where the timeline that has been constructed becomes a little fuzzy. The raids of Astra's premises that saw the seizure of *I Spit on Your Grave* did not take place until one week after the release of *Snuff* — begging the question, if Behr was confident enough to taunt authorities by asking 'what can they do about it?', then why would he seek legal advice one full week before he faced any legal issues over the release of *I Spit on Your Grave*?

A report covering the raid on Astra's premises stated categorically that Astra had chosen to withdraw *Snuff* before any cassettes found their way onto the market, contradicting Behr's earlier account that they had already sold 2500 copies on the first day of release. When the raid took place on June 9, 1982, *Snuff* had already been available for a little over a week. However, no copies of *Snuff* were found or confiscated during these raids. It is reasonable to assume that given the lead time in producing videos cassettes for distribution that the officers confiscating *I Spit on Your Grave* would have stumbled upon copies of *Snuff*, and given the contentious nature of the film might well have promptly confiscated *Snuff* as well. However, neither the report published in *Video Business* documenting the raid or a transcript of the official court report refer to anything other than *I Spit on Your Grave* (1982c).

The lack of reference to *Snuff* in any of this material could go some way in corroborating Behr's account that his company was not involved in the distribution of the film. He has always maintained that a piracy group had released the tape, yet there is no way to conclusively prove this. It could just as easily suggest that Astra Video, sensing the potential problems associated with the film, shrewdly arranged the production and/ or storage of the cassettes elsewhere. Certainly, by September 12, 1982, it was clear that *Snuff* had indeed made its way onto the market, when *The Sunday Times* reported that piracy rings dealing in 'nasties' were selling the problematic title. Behr maintained his innocence and suggested that his master copy of the tape had been sent back to the US before any copies of the film had been made. He claimed that the pirate copy of *Snuff* that he had seen and that was in circulation was 'not *Snuff* at all, but a compilation of various cuts under the snuff label' (Chippendale, 1982b), presumably suggesting that it was a compilation of violent material not unlike Astra's own *The Best of Sex and Violence*.

Nevertheless, and despite Behr's insistence to the contrary, the film had made its way on to the market, albeit in a slightly modified form. The content of the film itself remained unchanged from the American release, but the packaging displayed a marked difference from the original Astra promotional images that had been circulated to the press. The sky-blue border and background of Astra's original sleeve design had given way to a stark black design and all mention of Astra and its association with the product had been removed. The cassette label which would typically feature the logo of the company was not present, and instead, a distinctly amateur label appeared in its place. These elements, when combined with the fact that this black-sleeved version did not even feature the title of the film on the spine of the cover, lent an altogether more illicit sensibility to a film that Astra had intended to promote by far more conventional means. Behr's interview in *Shock Horror* reiterates a history in which Astra Video was not responsible for the release of *Snuff*, and while most reports from the period serve to corroborate his position, the timeline Behr has constructed around the release and its subsequent withdrawal does not hold up to scrutiny. The aforementioned article in *The Daily Express* clearly states that the company had already taken orders for 2500 units on the first day of release, indicating that the film was already available. When this is added to what seem to be erroneous claims of seeking legal counsel before encountering any legal issues, the official narrative appears unconvincing.

In June of 1982, *TV and Video Retailer* magazine published an article reporting on the Northern Software Show, a huge international trade fair that had taken place at Manchester's Excelsior Hotel in the previous month between the 23–25 of May (1982d: 52). The article reports that:

> Astra Video launched the controversial *Snuff* title at the show and trade appeared to be booming. This apparently uncensored film shows scenes of explicit violence, so we are told as Astra were refusing to preview the film on their stand.

While it is difficult to know how many copies they sold that day, it is useful to assess other titles in Astra's catalogue and their performance at previous trade fairs as a barometer. At the Software Show held in Heathrow near London earlier that same year, Astra's bestsellers were Wizard products, with Behr claiming that he had sold over 1000 units of *I Spit on Your Grave* and around 900 units of the John Landis film *Schlock* (1973). Factoring in the buzz that surrounded the release of *Snuff*, it would seem reasonable to assume that sales would have been comparable to the amount in Manchester. When this figure is combined with the 2500 units that had already sold, it really begins to muddy the claims that none of the videos had made it to market.

By February of 1983, *Video Viewer* magazine reported that, despite being unable to conclusively link Behr to the release, the DPP was still considering prosecuting Astra, simply for allowing copies of *Snuff* to be leaked onto the market (Anon, 1983). The article is illustrated using Astra's own artwork, replete with company logo and a blue-sleeved design, a design that was not employed in the black-sleeved 'bootlegs' that were now widely circulating. Behr continued to try to convince the DPP that he was not responsible for the release, maintaining that 'a well-known piracy ring' had produced and distributed the film.

Piracy was certainly a huge problem that the industry was facing throughout this period, but piracy, when defined in its strictest terms as the unauthorised reproduction and distribution of another individual or organisation's work for financial gain, is not wholly applicable here. The black-sleeved *Snuff* is not simply a reproduction; rather, it is a *re-appropriation*. It uses elements that were present in the original artwork while removing all reference to the distributor. The label again repeats this motif, removing all reference to Astra in favour of stark lettering of the title *Snuff* and the running time of the film. The motivation to redesign the sleeve and label in this manner calls into question the origin of the design. Why would a piracy gang redesign the product to remove reference to the distributor? Arguably, the only party that stood to benefit from the removal of the distribution details would be the distributor themselves, who wanted to profit from but simultaneously distance themselves from the film. However, whether or not Astra was responsible for this release is unclear. What we do know is that this was the version that was available from the time of its scheduled release, and it has continued to circulate among collectors for forty years. Deemed by many a bootleg, the black-sleeved version has paradoxically become regarded as authentic – a contemporaneous copy which for many years was the only version available and has therefore been given an imprimatur of authenticity.

BLUE-SLEEVED *SNUFF*

This overview of *Snuff*'s already confused distribution is littered with enough inconsistencies and discrepancies that it has afforded space for speculation and debate surrounding the circulation of the film for fans and collectors who are keen to understand the nuances of the film's distribution history. However, this narrative is confused even further by the existence of a second release that only came to light in the late 1990s. This version outwardly appeared to be the official release produced by Astra Video. Blue-sleeved *Snuff*, as it became known, utilises the original artwork from Astra and bears the logo of both Astra and Cult Video, the imprint of Astra's American partner, Wizard. Alongside this, the sleeve clearly states that it had been 'printed in the U.S.A', mirroring other Wizard/Cult Video collaborations of the same period.

Scepticism about the provenance of the release has led to the cover, label and stock of the tape being scrutinised and these inconsistencies have cast enough doubt over the legitimacy of the release that is largely regarded as bootleg. Consensus has it that this bootleg was produced much later in an effort to deceive collectors by capitalising on the authenticity of the official artwork in an effort to dupe unwitting fans into thinking that this was the mythical 'official' release. However, and as with most of *Snuff*'s 'history' much of this is speculative, enough concerns have been raised over the provenance of the blue-sleeved version that it has led to a ban on all sales of the cassette on the Pre-Certification Video forum (www.pre-cert.co.uk), a hub for collectors of 'pre-cert' videos, until new information comes to light that can legitimate the release.

Since the image of the sleeve had been widely circulated to the British press in a promotional campaign used in the run up to the release of the film, scepticism surrounding the legitimacy of the blue-sleeved version is understandable. Behr had claimed that 'Charles Band, the rights owner, probably shipped them (the sleeves) to Belgium, and that further illicit copies entered the UK from there', but this seems unlikely and is another element of the narrative that is largely refuted by collectors (Brewster, Fenton and Morris, 2005). Andy Allard, one of the regular contributors to the Pre-Certification Video discussion forum, suggests in a comprehensive overview of the history of the blue-sleeved variant that the 'first verified appearance dates to the late 90s with more appearing via eBay and trade lists, and a number of known dodgy copies, in the 2000s' (2010). The desire to weed out the 'dodgy copies' has led 'Hellochas', a moderator on the forum, to conduct a comparative analysis of the known copies in circulation among members of the site. By scrutinising printing defects common to the sleeve of many of the known copies of the blue-sleeved version, he was able to determine that the known copies were reproduced from a single master that contained these imperfections. In August 2022, a member of a Facebook group dedicated to

Fig. 7

pre-cert collecting posted an unfolded sleeve for blue-sleeved *Snuff* that he had bought from eBay in 2016, complete with staple holes, evidently the master sleeve from which the blue sleeve duplicates were made. This indicates that these are indeed products of an unscrupulous collector seeking to capitalise on the 'authenticity' of the original sleeve, though debate will like continue. But it also highlights, unequivocally, the importance of legitimacy to the community.

THE AUTHENTICITY OF *SNUFF*

While this discussion of the attention to detail around the minutiae of these releases may seem inconsequential, what lies at the heart of these debates is a question over the authenticity of *Snuff* and the significance of this information to the collector's market that has grown up around 'video nasties'. These debates seek to validate either of the two available versions: the black-sleeved version and the blue-sleeved version. While the similarities between the releases are immediately apparent (the same image as a basis for the design and the same hyperbolic text and bold typography), it is the differences that have become the basis for most debate among collectors. These range from the absence of the film's title on the spine or even a named distributor on the black-sleeved version, to the printing imperfections evident in the blue-sleeved version. Even the kerning of the text on the cassette labels has been scrutinised in attempts to prove or disprove the validity of either version.

These cassettes are now forty years old and are increasingly understood as important cultural artefacts, in much in the same way that first editions of books are afforded importance as collectors' items (for a detailed examination of the culture of collecting that surrounds the 'video nasties', refer to Kate Egan, 2007). The pre-certification releases of the 'video nasties' are valued and are valuable. They are perhaps doubly significant in this regard, as they are at once first editions, the first releases of the films on video, augmented by a further scarcity as a result of their inclusion in a catalogue of banned films that were removed from circulation and destroyed by the authorities.

Since the demise of VHS technology and, subsequently, the decline in popularity of physical media altogether, there has been increased interest in what Charles R. Acland has referred to as 'residual media' forms (see Acland, 2006). Russell W. Belk has suggested that the 'two core characteristics of any mass-produced objects [that] make them suitable for collecting [are] seriality and (lack of) abundance' (2001: 35). In the case of the 'video nasties', the seriality can be seen as a result of the films inclusion in the DPP banned film list, while the lack of abundance is as a result of the criminalisation of the cassettes, and their removal and destruction at the hands of the DPP. This history is important for many reasons, not least because it introduced a draconian system of censorship to the British marketplace. However, in doing so it also inadvertently created a series of collectibles that are only becoming more valuable as the years progress. Collectors of the 'video nasties' are understandably invested in the legitimacy of the artefact, and, as with any market geared towards the aficionado or specialist, value is ascribed to objects based upon any number of different factors, not least, scarcity.

The importance placed upon these videos by collectors and enthusiasts is just one aspect of a complex narrative that is filled with conflicting accounts, speculation and misinformation.

Fig. 8

Complicating the story somewhat is an auction that took place on eBay in November 2013. The seller, Graham Foley, was auctioning what appeared to be an original poster for the UK video release of *Snuff*. The poster displayed the damage commensurate with its age – nicks, tears and fading – and crucially, featured all of the elements of the black-sleeved design but with two vitally important additions – the logos for both Wizard and Astra Video. The auction was unsuccessful due largely to the condition of the poster, an elevated reserve price, and speculation from some collectors that it simply could not be genuine since Astra had never officially released the film. For others, the appearance of a poster that incorporated the logos of Astra and Wizard onto the black-sleeved design proved unequivocally that Astra was indeed behind the bootleg all along. One member of the Pre-Certification Video forum suggested that, because Astra's initial promotion campaign had featured the blue-sleeved version of the tape, he would have expected the poster found on eBay to have been publicising the blue-sleeved version of *Snuff*; the fact that it did not, encouraged him and others to consider it 'proof that Astra were [sic] behind the black sleeve release' (Hellochas, 2013).

These ongoing debates suggest that, for these collectors, there is an investment that transcends the simple acquisition of the object and moves into areas in which they can interpret the history that has been constructed. Here, within this community, collectors pool their knowledge which is then analysed in terms of its validity in relation to the other *verifiable* parts of the history that has been constructed. This is an ongoing discussion that affords collectors a space in which to scrutinise the most contested parts of that history while contributing to its ongoing examination. Significantly, this process casts collectors as archivists, as custodians and as historians. A simple search for *Snuff* on the Pre-Certification Video forum returns 648 threads containing thousands of posts, with many of these threads dedicated entirely to the debates that persist around this release. From the individual desire to solve the 'mystery' of *Snuff*'s release to the sharing of knowledge within the community, or even to the less altruistic, but no less important, motivation to simply assessing the monetary value of any given version, there is a continued investment from collectors into this release.

This troubled distribution history of *Snuff* in the UK and its fragmented circulation as a video cassette has provided the film with a curious, sensational afterlife that exists far beyond the debates about the authenticity of the 'murder'. However, I would argue that the decision by Astra to distance itself from the release while largely motivated by fear of repercussions, has allowed space for a mythology to evolve which has enabled the idea of snuff to permeate the popular consciousness in the UK in a way that an official traceable history would not. If Astra, or any distributor for that matter, had come forward to claim ownership of the distribution of *Snuff*, it would have turned what has always been presented as an intangible external threat into a less exotic internal threat, a threat that was likely created at Astra Video's offices in Croydon. It would have led to more focussed reports that would have been forced to wrestle with the reality, that Snuff, for all of the sensational claims of the advertising campaign, was not a real snuff movie. It would have apportioned blame to Astra and the threat that *Snuff* posed would have been minimised and evaporated under the realisation that the film was a hoax. However, with no distributor to take account for the claims that were being made about *Snuff*, those not invested in either the film or 'video nasties' more generally could speculate on the reality of the snuff movie.

Chapter 4. The Legacy of *Snuff*

Since 2017, and the release of Jordan Peele's Oscar-winning directorial debut *Get Out*, there has been a discursive shift that has sought to elevate what are being presented as a radically new wave of 'important' horror films in a re-evaluation that often comes at the expense of early examples of the genre. William Proctor (2018) has followed these claims of a horror 'renaissance' (Evans, 2017) and 'golden age' (Hess, 2017) and suggests that much of this discourse is based upon the misguided belief that the horror film has always 'been unquestionably fringe, unmistakably cult, emphatically marginal and wholly disparaged', something which Proctor rejects. Instead, he argues that horror cinema, like other genres, is perhaps better understood as 'less a coherent category than [...] a system of currents, cycles and trends' (2018), suggesting that what this resurgence reveals is the frequency with which the industry returns to this kind of discursive ballyhoo as a means of repositioning the genre. While recently this repositioning has been articulated through ideas of quality and significance, historically, these conversations would have focussed explicitly upon the perceived extremity of the films.

This emphasis on excess was perhaps best articulated by David Edelstein in 2006, when he expressed concern over a genre that he felt was revelling in 'explicit scenes of torture and mutilation' (Edelstein, 2006). In a now-famous article for *New York Magazine*, Edelstein identified what he felt was a new wave of horror films, 'torture porn', a category into which he included *Hostel* (2005), *The Devil's Rejects* (2005), *Saw* (2004), *Wolf Creek* (2005), and even *The Passion of the Christ* (2004). Edelstein claimed that he was a horror connoisseur and suggested that he had long since made peace with the genre's inherent sadism but could not understand the popularity of these new films that seem to revel in scenes of torture and dismemberment. However, despite Edelstein's protestations, if he truly were invested in the history of horror then he would have recognised the traditions on which these films were drawing.

In his exploration of the so-called torture porn cycle of films, Steve Jones has suggested that what Edelstein had actually highlighted was simply the most visible strand of a commercially profitable genre, arguing that much of 'contemporary American hardcore horror adheres to a visual style that is fashioned after the mythic "snuff" film' (2013: 174-5). For Jones, the genre exists on a continuum, and while *Hostel*, *The Devil's Rejects* and *Wolf Creek* might represent the most commercially successful branch of that genre, there is another branch of underground horror filmmaking that runs in parallel to these films. Here, Jones highlights Fred Vogel's controversial 'August Underground' series and Lucifer Valentine's 'Vomit Gore' trilogy, as notable examples of contemporary films that rework the aesthetic of the snuff film, though often to a far more gratuitous effect. These are niche films that exist far beyond the commercial canon. They are often presented as degraded home movies and, with little narrative to speak of, play with the idea of the snuff movie. These films owe a considerable debt to both the myth of snuff and to the film itself, revelling in a homemade aesthetic that claims to present footage of real murder. However, while the films of Valentine and Vogel are directly indebted to *Snuff*, they represent only the most marginal and fringe aspects of an idea that has impacted immeasurably on popular culture.

The central thesis of *Snuff* has been reworked so many times, in so many different films, and in so many different contexts that it is impossible to know just how important a cinematic legacy *Snuff* really has. It can perhaps be seen most visibly in Paul Schrader's *Hardcore* (1979), with an idea that was later reworked into Joel Schumacher's crime drama *8mm* (1999). It can be seen in the cycle of 'Mondo' movies that begins in earnest in 1978 with the notorious pseudo-documentary series *Faces of Death* (1978-1995). It can also be seen in the spiritual successor to this series, *Traces of Death* (1993-2000; see Walker, 2016). It can be seen in Ruggero Deodato's seminal Mondo-inspired progenitor of the found-footage genre, *Cannibal Holocaust* (1980), and in the Japanese Guinea Pig series of films, the most notorious of which inspired an FBI investigation after the actor Charlie Sheen became convinced that he had actually witnessed a real murder. It can be seen in Srđan Spasojević's hugely controversial *A Serbian Film* (2010) and the ideas have even been reworked for television – in John Carpenter's 'Cigarette Burns' episode of *Masters of Horror* (2005), in which a crazed director attempts to murder an angel on camera, and in 'The Devil of Christmas' (2016), an episode in the British anthology series *Inside Number 9*, at the end of which an actress realises the low-budget shocker she's been starring in as a pregnant bride is an extended set-up for her own violent murder, in what may be a nod to Sharon Tate's murder and the origins of the snuff myth.

However, while the narrative tropes and aesthetic of *Snuff* are evident across film and television, the legacy of the film cannot be reduced to the ways that the film has impacted on cinema, popular or otherwise. *Snuff* contributed to the still widely-held belief in the existence of the snuff movie, and in that, the film has had far-reaching political implications far beyond the narrow purview of a little-seen exploitation film. This chapter will examine the cultural and political legacy of *Snuff* and will attempt to assess the impact of the film since its release in 1976.

THE CULTURAL LEGACY OF *SNUFF*

The most enduring aspect of the legacy of *Snuff* is the way that it contributed to the still widely held belief in the production of the commercial snuff movie. These ideas are still with us and can be seen in the coverage of some of the most horrific crimes imaginable. In 2018 radical feminist and co-founder of the law reform group Justice for Women, Julie Bindel, published an article in *The Independent* about the horrific murder of the Swedish journalist Kim Wall, attributing it to the apparent pervasiveness of snuff movies (Bindel, 2018). On 10 August 2017, Wall had boarded the UC3 Nautilus, a midget submarine built by Danish entrepreneur, Peter Madsen, to interview Madsen about his invention. When she failed to return home, Wall's boyfriend reported her missing and a search to find her began in the early hours of the following day. When Madsen was found he insisted that the submarine had suffered a technical failure and had sunk to the bottom of the ocean, but that he had dropped Wall off near Copenhagen before that had happened.

The search continued and, ten days later, Wall's torso was discovered by a passing cyclist washed up on a beach south of Copenhagen. On 6 October, Wall's legs, clothes and a knife were found in two plastic bags, then on 21 and 29 November, Wall's arms were found in the bay (Orange, 2018). During Madsen's trial the prosecution heard from witnesses who claimed that prior to the murder, Madsen had become obsessed with watching 'beheading videos, practised asphyxiation sex and was fascinated by sex and death' (Orange, 2017). It was later revealed that he had searched the internet for 'beheaded girl agony' just hours before he met with Wall (Malm, 2018), and it was presumably because of this that Julie Bindel argued that Madsen was inspired to murder by what she saw as a worrying trend towards brutal, sadistic and misogynistic pornography which culminated in murder – the snuff movie.

Bindel claimed that she had seen the kind of pornography that had inspired Madsen to murder in the 1980s, insisting that together with a group of anti-porn activists, journalists and experts in special effects, she had seen the elusive snuff movie. Bindel claimed that 'one of the activists had gone into a porn shop in England and asked if the owner had something "really extreme"', and she claims the storeowner gave them the film of 'a woman in South America being raped, tortured and murdered', and that they 'saw her hand sawn off while she was still alive' (Bindel, 2018). She goes on to suggest that 'even the hardened crime reporters had to leave the room to be sick', but that the feminists stayed because they knew what to expect, as they had heard about snuff from activists in the US who were campaigning against the torture and murder of women for men's sexual pleasure. These American activists were no doubt the same group who had protested the original theatrical release of *Snuff*, Andrea Dworkin, Susan Brownmiller, and the Women Against Violence Against Women (WAVAW) network, and while Brownmiller had later conceded that the rumours of real murder had been greatly exaggerated, many of her colleagues, Dworkin and Bindel included, simply doubled down on their belief and refused any such concession. With tales of snuff films being imported from South America and hands being cut off living victims, it seems as if Bindel's is describing the film *Snuff*, rather than a 'legitimate' snuff movie, but despite this, she has never wavered in her belief. In her 2018 interview for *The Independent*, Bindel reworked a story that she has told many times before, most notably in *The Guardian* way back in 2006. Where she argued:

> Twenty-five years ago I watched a snuff movie with other anti-porn activists, journalists and special film-effects experts. One of the activists had gone into a porn shop in England and asked if the owner had something 'really extreme'. He gave her a film of a woman in South America being raped, tortured and murdered. As a finale, her hand was sawn off. By that time it was only the feminists left in the room, the others having run out to cry, or be sick. We knew what we would be seeing, because we had heard about it from activists in the US who were fighting the same battles.
>
> We had proved that snuff existed (the film experts verified that there were no camera tricks to depict the sawing), and one of the journalists wrote copiously about the issue, urging police to take action. Nothing happened.

While much of the same language is repeated in the article published in *The Independent*, there is one additional piece of information that was missing from the earlier article which helps us to date the screening. Here Bindel suggests that twenty-five years prior to 2006 she was witness to a real snuff movie. This would place the screening around 1981/1982, just as home video was finding a foothold in the UK. It's therefore possible, if not likely, that screening took place on or after May of 1982, after the scheduled release of *Snuff* by Astra Video. While Bindel suggests that 'one of the journalists wrote copiously about the issue, urging the police to take action', this does not seem to be present in national coverage, and her suggestion that 'nothing happened' is patently not true in the case of *Snuff*. As demonstrated in the previous chapter, *Snuff* became the myth that underpinned an entire campaign, resulting in prosecutions and custodial sentences, and ushering in a wave of censorship. This is hardly insignificant, but nor is it the proof that snuff movies existed, as Bindel had claimed.

Glenn Ward challenged Bindel's 2006 article, arguing that the 'recourse to the entire South American subcontinent is as vague and homogenizing as that of Shackleton', and in the absence of any real evidence, relies on the readers' preconceptions of the South American snuff myth (2009: 149). Significantly, despite Bindel's account having many detractors, when the question of its accuracy was raised on the *Reddit* group r/GenderCritical, the idea of the existence of snuff was still greeted favourably. The group describes itself as 'a women-centered, radical feminist subreddit to discuss gender from a critical, feminist perspective'. While there was some debate amongst contributors, most concluded that the likelihood of snuff's existence should act as proof of its existence, with one user suggesting that if 'we know men kidnap, torture, rape, and murder women ... and we know they film us in pain for their own pleasure... we know they film child rape!! Is it so farfetched that there are sadists out there filming their murders?'. Some argued that the current definition for what might constitute a snuff film was too restrictive (an idea that I will return to in the final chapter), suggesting that it omitted films which, while not produced solely and specifically with the intention of selling for profit, could be later repurposed as a commercial snuff film. Others cautioned against the inclusion of any and all murders caught on film, as they failed to meet the textbook definition of a snuff movie.[3] However, despite a failure to reach a consensus, the dominant perspective articulated on the thread was that not only did snuff movies exist but that they were also incredibly common, readily available over the dark web and through websites like 4Chan. Nobody provided links to any evidence of snuff movies as proof, instead reiterating the cornerstone of the snuff myth, that it was decidedly foreign, arriving in the country from elsewhere.

As Ward highlights in relation to Bindel's article, narratives of this type simply rework the promotional material for Shackleton's *Snuff*, in its suggestion that it was 'made in South America where life is cheap!'. However, while the myth often tells of snuff movies being made in South America, the narrative continues to be reworked from country to country as a means of localising the threat and bolstering the narrative. In North America these crimes were being reported as being committed in South America; in the UK, they were reported as coming from Amsterdam; WAVAW believed that the films were arriving from California (Thompson, 1994: 90); while the Reddit group mentioned above believed that much of modern-day snuff originates in Cambodia and Serbia – though, again, no evidence is provided to back-up any of these claims. The latter is likely inspired by the notoriety of Spasojević's controversial *A Serbian Film*, and the mention of Cambodia conflates snuff with the no-less horrific crime of filmed paedophilic abuse videos, which, while clearly horrendous, do not constitute snuff in the traditional sense of the word. Instead, what seems to happen is that it becomes an argument about 'common sense', where the burden of proof is on sceptics to prove that snuff does not exist, rather than the other way around.

Bindel insisted that prior to the screening of *Snuff*, many 'porn apologists' had argued that snuff did not exist, believing that feminists had invented the story to add weight to their anti-porn campaign, but that they had since 'proved the sceptics wrong' (Bindel, 2018). However, with no record of who attended this screening, or who these supposed film experts were, there is no evidence to corroborate Bindel's insistence on the existence of the snuff movie. Despite this, there is no shortage of people willing to believe in their existence or indeed claim that they have seen a snuff movie. Indeed, someone who may have been in attendance at Bindel's screening is Irish campaigner, Clodagh Corcoran, who similarly recalled her experience of viewing a snuff film in the early 1980s, in *Pornography: The New Terrorism* (1989: 4):

> I want to describe it to you in detail. But I cannot, because my mind won't let me.

What I can tell you is that on that night I watched a man participate in the act of sex with a woman, and during that act he plunged a large hunting knife into her stomach and cut her open from vagina to breast. He then withdrew the knife and stuck it into her left hand, removing the first three joints from her fingers, which fell from the bed. The woman's eyes remained open, she looked at the knife and said 'Oh God, not me'. It took her approximately three minutes to die. The camera was left running. The film was then canned and put on the commercial market as entertainment.

Though some of the details seem to have been hyperbolically reworked for effect, Corcoran's account, much like Bindel, appears to be describing the coda to *Snuff*, in which the victim's fingers are removed with pliers, and then a knife plunged is into her stomach. However, unlike Bindel, Corcoran claimed to have evidence of the snuff movie and was booked to participate in a press conference about pornography and censorship and had arranged to screen the film for the audience who were in attendance. She claims that this didn't happen because of faulty equipment, but insists that ever since she saw the film, she has lived in fear 'knowing that while the rape, degradation and dehumanisation of women is filmed and sold as entertainment, women's status in society is worthless' (1989: 4). Corcoran takes things further by insisting that hardcore pornography routinely showed 'flaying, cannibalism, [...] exploding vaginas packed with hand grenades, eyes gouged out, [...] dismemberings, and burnings, multiple rape, [...] the films of real rapes by rapists and the actual killing of women is easily, readily and illegally, frequently obtained from under the counter or the back room of the second-hand magazine sellers and many, many video shops' (1989: 6). However, as compelling and significant as this revelatory report might seem, it is very similar to a quotation from Catherine Itzin's article from the previous year: 'Sex and Censorship: The Political Implications' (1988). Itzin attributes the quote to journalist Polly Toynbee, who, writing for *The Guardian* on 30 October 1981, described the same 'scenes of castration, cannibalism, flaying, the crushing of breasts in vices, exploding vaginas packed with hand grenades, eyes gouged out, beatings, dismemberings, burnings, multiple rape and every other horror that could befall the human body' (Toynbee, quoted in Itzen, 1988). However, Toynbee's report has been used here to conflate scenes of fictionalised violence which were staged for dramatic effect, with scenes of actual violence, in which actual harm befell the performers on the screen. Toynbee had been a member of what became known as the Williams' Committee, the Committee on Obscenity and Film Censorship that was appointed on 13 July 1977. Chaired by Professor Bernard Williams, from whom the group took its name, the Committee was formed with the purpose of reviewing 'the laws concerning obscenity, indecency and violence in publications, displays and entertainments in England and Wales, [...] and to review the arrangements for film censorship in England and Wales; and to make recommendations' (Williams Committee, 1979: 3). Because of the interest in film, the committee met with James Ferman, then secretary of the British Board of Film Censors (as it was at the time), who spent four afternoons explaining the Board's policy and practice (Williams Committee, 1979: 5). The report details that over the course of those four afternoons, Ferman showed the Committee extracts from ninety different films, often in 'before' and 'after' versions, as a way of illustrating the strategy employed by the Board in their decision to censor the depiction of violence, the depiction of sex, and the depiction of sexual violence. Of those ninety films, the Committee was particularly interested in viewing some films in their entirety. These included films that had previously caused controversy after they had been approved for release by the Board: *Straw Dogs* (1971), *A Clockwork Orange* (1971) and *The Language of Love* (1969), were screened alongside films where the censor had withheld a certificate and had been criticised by some for doing so: *The Story of O* (1975), Pier Paolo Pasolini's *Salò* (1975), Nagisa Oshima's *Empire of the Senses* (1976) and Louis Malle's *Pretty Baby* (1978), and, ironically perhaps, given the relationship of the snuff myth to the Manson murders, the documentary film *Manson* (1972). Although *Manson* was not violent, it had been refused a certificate in 1972 because it was felt that the film could incite violence. The published report makes no reference to the kind of violence that Toynbee described, although it does acknowledge the persistence of the belief in snuff:

> There have been instances in which the alleged harm to participants has fallen in a very different category. It has been suggested, for example, that there is a genre of film—the so-called 'snuff' movie—usually said to originate in South America, in which sadistic pornography is taken to the obscenity and film censorship extreme of having an unsuspecting model actually mutilated and murdered in front of the camera. There has been much scepticism about the existence of films of this kind and although rumours about their existence were indeed followed in America by the appearance

of a film called *Snuff* ('the film that could only be made in South America ... where life is cheap!') there appeared to be general agreement that the violence in the film was simulated rather than real; it is possible that the rumours themselves had been engineered for the purposes of advance publicity for this film. Another film, which we saw, which purported to include actual documentary sequences of mutilation and death, was subsequently reported to have been, at least in part, faked.
(Williams Committee, 1999: 120)

While it is likely that the second film mentioned here was the similarly controversial *Faces of Death* (1978), a film that merged news reel footage with dramatic reconstructions to horrific effect, it is clear that the committee held little stock in the actual existence of the snuff movie, even going as far as to attribute the belief that these films originated in South America to Shackleton's pervasive publicity campaign. However, despite the findings of the Committee, it was Toynbee's description in *The Guardian* that has gone on to garner the most attention about the possibility of the existence of snuff and, perhaps more worryingly, continues to be reprinted as evidence of the existence of snuff, gaining further credibility when it was incorporated into the policy statement for the Campaign Against Pornography and Censorship.

> We also believe that pornography includes what is called 'hardcore' pornography: torture, flaying, cannibalism, crushing of breasts in vices, exploding vaginas packed with hand-grenades, eyes gouged out, beatings, dismemberings, and burnings, multiple rape, women engaged in sexual intercourse with animals, the filming of real rapes by rapists and the actual killing of women on screen in 'snuff' films. (Smith, 1993)

The coordinator for the Campaign Against Pornography and Censorship was Catherine Itzin, the author of 'Sex and Censorship', who reprinted Toynbee's original account and in doing so gave credence to the myth. The statement has continued to gain traction, reprinted in Anne Glyn-Jones' *Holding Up a Mirror: How Civilisations Decline* (1996: 462), a critique of contemporary society in which she takes these ideas not just as evidence of the existence of snuff, but as one of the markers of the decline of Western civilisation. In the narrative that Glyn-Jones constructs, she suggests that in 1979 a poster for a film called 'Snuff' began circulating which claimed that the final scene 'showed a woman being killed and her uterus ripped out' (1996: 463). Again, the source of this information was

Itzen, and it seems to conflate the misreported aspects of the Manson murders with the narrative of Shackleton's conclusion to *Snuff*, and the convergence of these histories can be seen over and over again. A document in the archives of Mary Whitehouse and the National Viewers and Listeners Association suggests that snuff movies were apparently prevalent in Colchester (where Whitehouse lived) and, just as in the USA, imagines them a decidedly foreign threat, only this time arriving in the UK from Amsterdam.

> One film showed a young fourteen year old girl being cut up into little pieces. Coming into the country from Amsterdam on the boats usually the 24 hour day trip. Coming through with the Personnel Staff in pockets, handbags, luggage even Duty Free Bags belonging to staff not searched Sold for around £80 from car boots etc. They have approached shops but shops were not interested. Films are in Colchester and quite a lot of child sex film have been offered – sold. Originating from U.S.A. The 'Family' were mentioned.
>
> (Anon, Clippings file, Archives of the National Viewers and Listeners Association, Albert Sloman Library, University of Essex)

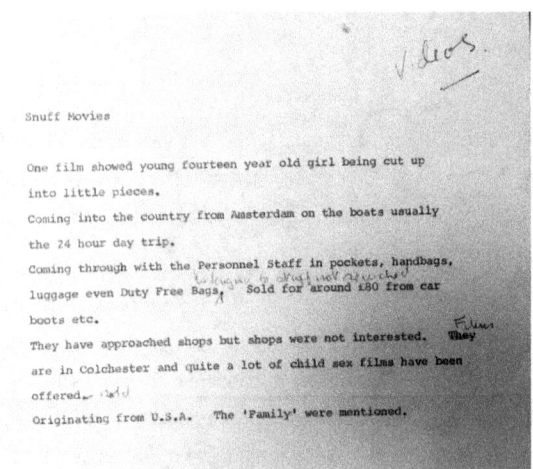

Fig. 9

The suggestion that the films were entering the UK from Amsterdam clearly invokes Shackleton's narrative of South America, insisting on a foreign 'other' of whom we should be afraid; while the assertion that the films originate in the United States and were produced by 'The Family' illustrates just how reliant the narrative of snuff movies was on the crimes of the 'Manson family'. These elements are frequently conflated in a way that has allowed the mythology of the snuff movie to thrive.

While this is the cultural legacy of *Snuff* in a British context, the film, understandably, has very different connotations and a very different legacy in South America. It is here that *The Slaughter* was filmed, and it is from here that the snuff myth originates, at least according to *The New York Times*. Moreover, when Shackleton decided to capitalise on these rumours he did so through rhetoric that presented the entire South American subcontinent as a vague and homogenized imaginary. For all of these reasons, *Snuff* has very different legacy in South America and the final section of this chapter will explore this legacy and consider the implications of Shackleton's campaign.

THE CULTURAL LEGACY OF *SNUFF* IN SOUTH AMERICA

Shackleton's decision to market *Snuff* as a film 'made in South America, where life is cheap', while undeniably effective, carries with it the weight of an entire generation who were tortured in a regime of state-sponsored terrorism. This forces us to confront some of the more troubling aspects of the legacy of *Snuff* in a South American context. Argentina has a troubled political history, with the country suffering under the regimes of extremists from both the left and the right (see Romero, 2002). In 1976, a right-wing coup successfully deposed President Isabel Perón, resulting in the military seizing control of the government and forming a dictatorship that they called the National Reorganization Process (NRP). Under the banner of the NRP, the dictatorship began eradicating society of students, militants, trade unionists, writers, journalists, artists – indeed, any citizen that they suspected of being involved with left-wing activities. The NRP was part of a United States-backed, continent-wide campaign known as Operation Condor, the purpose of which was to rid Argentina, Bolivia, Brazil, Chile, Paraguay, Uruguay, and to a lesser degree Colombia, Peru and Venezuela of any left-wing opposition, targeting anyone who might oppose the institution of new economic neoliberal policies (Blakeley, 2009:22). In Argentina, this was achieved through a sustained campaign of state-sanctioned terrorism that lasted from 1976 until 1983.

Known as 'the Dirty War', this ruthless campaign of violence took the lives of almost 30,000 people, with the government actively abducting, torturing, and assassinating anyone it deemed a problem. Marguerite Feitlowitz documents that the 'victims died during torture, were machine-gunned at the edge of enormous pits, or were thrown, drugged, from airplanes into the sea' and that these individuals became known as 'the missing' (Feitlowitz, 2011: IX).

The government would also assassinate known communists and rehome their children with military families who supported their cause, leading to a generation that was forcibly adopted and estranged from their own families. Beginning in 1977, and assembling every year since, mothers and grandmothers of these children bravely gathered at the Plaza de Mayo in Buenos Aires, in front of the presidential palace, flouting repressive governmental policies that forbade mass assembly and demanding the return of their children, who had become known as 'the disappeared'. This was the culture on which Shackleton was commenting when he took the decision to capitalise on the rumours of snuff movies arriving from South America, and while his exploitation of the political situation made for memorable advertising copy, for obvious reasons, the film has very different meanings and associations for those who were forced to live through the National Reorganization Process.

In 2015, Joaquín Aras, an artist and filmmaker from Buenos Aires began exploring some of those meanings when he unveiled his latest work; a project funded by the Bienal de Arte Joven de Buenos Aires that considered issues of cultural memory, film history, and film preservation, and that, crucially, used *Snuff* as means of exploring these ideas. *Snuff 1976* is a video installation that attempts to modify the meanings and associations of the film by presenting the film from an Argentinian perspective. For Aras, the film is a symbolic reflection of the violence of the Dirty War and his work offers a commentary that finds parallels between the war and the production of *Snuff*.

Aras argues that because modern-day Argentina is a relatively young country, with its roots in Spanish colonization and the decimation of the indigenous population by the conquistadors, the Argentine people have never really had a relationship with history in which they knew how to preserve it (Aras, 2019). As an example of this, he cites the desecration of one of the most important buildings in Argentina, the Cabildo de Buenos

Aires. The building contains the National Museum of the Cabildo, and before the May Revolution (1810) it was home to the Spanish Viceroy. It was used as the City Hall, and it was here, following an eight-year war, that Argentina proclaimed its independence from Spain. However, despite all its historical significance, between 1889 and 1931 several of the original columns and façades were removed to make room for two major roads.

For Aras, this act of vandalism illustrates the difficult relationship that Argentina has had with its own history, suggesting that this is a fragmented history that is markedly different from that of European countries. It is a history that has been

> Broken to pieces and put back together again, with conquests along the way, declarations of independence, waves of migration, coups and crises – again and again these moments in which past is erased and a new account of the history comes in, as well as another idea of the future that never managed to catch on. (Aras, 2020)

For Aras, the production of *Snuff* is a similarly fragmented history that has only ever been told from a North American or European perspective in publications which, much like this one, are primarily interested in cult film.

There are different kinds of violence depicted within the film *Snuff*, and while it is the violence in Shackleton's hyperbolic conclusion that has historically dominated discussion, for Aras these debates are overshadowed by the implicit violence of Shackleton's decision to remove the credits of the actors who appeared in the film. For Aras, and a generation of Argentinians who had mourned 'the missing' and 'the disappeared', the removal of these names represents another act of violence. In a film that purports to show images of real murder, and that trades upon rhetoric that invokes a period of huge political unrest and violence in South America and a regime that was bankrolled by North America, the idea that North American directors would come to South America to film and capitalise on this situation for financial gain is perhaps the ultimate exploitation. Aras details that:

> None of [the actors] spoke English, they signed no contracts, and there was no script. Some of the cast had to do their lines phonetically, others directly in Spanish. Dubbing then took place back in the US. The actresses never saw the finished film, and until I

went to see them, nobody had ever asked them about it. (2015)

Aras suggests that Argentinian history is full of losses and absences and that for him, the film *Snuff* had become symbolic of those absences. Just as many of the population had disappeared under the rule of the right-wing death squads, the Argentinian actors who had originally performed in *Snuff* had also 'disappeared', effectively removed from history. By reuniting the original cast Aras hoped to use the visual arts as a way of challenging dominant narratives and offering an alternative history that simultaneously commented on cultural memory in Argentina.

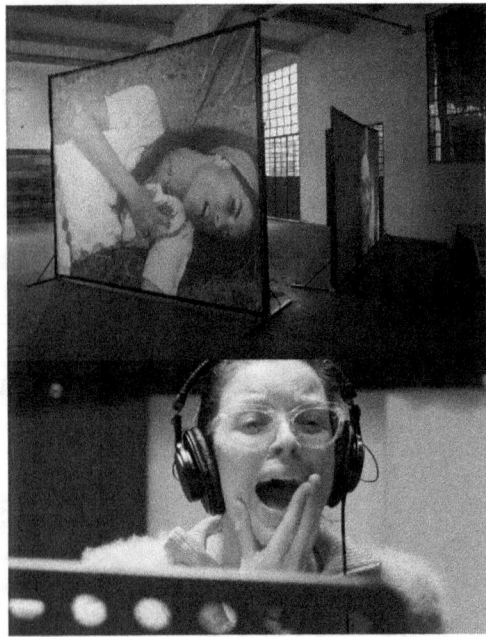

Fig. 10

Snuff 1976 brought together the actors to produce an Argentinian remake of the only part of the film that was not made in Argentina – the soundtrack. Recording the entire audio track of *Snuff* – the vocal tracks, music and sound effects – the film sought to return the film 'to its original context and in some way to repatriate the film' (Aras, 2015). This reworking of *Snuff* concludes with Margarita Amuchástegui, the actress who had played Angelica in the film, stating that 'the actors that worked in the film *Snuff* were not injured or harmed. The deaths in the film are not real they are part of a work of fiction,' commenting on and undermining Shackleton's hyperbolic claims. However, and perhaps most importantly in this context, Aras reinstates the credit sequence documenting the contributions of Roberta and Michael Findlay, Simon Nuctern for his work on the closing sequence, and most importantly, the actors – Margarita Amuchástegui, Ana Carro, Liliana Fernández Blanco, Alfredo Iglesias, Enrique Larratelli, Mirta Massa, Aldo Mayo, Clao Villanueva and Xanthe Ellis – and in doing so symbolically returns Argentina's 'disappeared'.

FOOTNOTES

3. In December of 2020, *The Atlantic* reported that the r/GenderCritical group had been removed from Reddit, banned as trans-exclusionary radical feminists (see Kaitlyn, 2020).

Chapter 5. The Reality and Redefinition of *Snuff*

While the imagined aesthetic of snuff is irrevocably tied to analogue technology and an aesthetic common to twentieth-century media, in reality and in the twenty-first century, the actual aesthetic of snuff is far more likely to be a high-definition digital presentation that is circulated via 'Tube' sites online. In an era that has democratised processes of production and broadcast, increased access to video recording technology through smartphones, webcams and other digital video platforms has not only increased the likelihood of snuff being produced, but it has also increased the likelihood these videos will be shared freely online across the internet. As seen in the previous chapter, claims continue to resurface about the existence of snuff movies, usually attached to horrific crimes of torture, rape and murder, which work to lend credibility to these stories. However, these claims never hold up to scrutiny or conform to the FBI definition of what constitutes a snuff movie.

Though most of the claims about the existence of snuff have concentrated on the torture of women on camera, it is the murder of a man by another man that presents the most visible challenge to the mythical status of the snuff movie. The tragic real-life murder of Jun Lin by the Canadian cannibal killer Luka Magnotta forces us to confront how the changing nature of economics, engagement and distribution have gradually eroded the ideas that were central to the FBI's definition, and in doing so, may have facilitated the production of the first genuine snuff movie. However, in order to fully understand how the murder of Jun Lin challenges traditional notions of the snuff movie, it is essential to first understand both the market that exists for material of this kind, and the ways in which Magnotta himself benefited from the production of this film.

The prevailing belief has always been that for a film to qualify as a snuff movie then the killing must be financially motivated and the film must circulate via illegal underground networks, changing hands for enormous sums of money between a community of deviants who derived sexual pleasure from watching someone die on camera. *1 Lunatic 1 Icepick*, and the footage of the murder of Jun Lin, does not conform to either of these criteria. It did not circulate via some underground network, and it did not appear on the 'Dark Web'. Instead, it circulated freely on social media and on easily accessible websites that were not hidden behind some covert paywall. The film was not shared for the sexual gratification of its audience, but it circulated instead for more complex reasons that tell us more about engagement with challenging media in the twenty-first century than it does about the supposed deviance of those who would watch this kind of material. The benefits to Magnotta cannot not be measured simply in terms of monetary value, but he was emboldened and enabled by the possibilities afforded him by the internet, and arguably, by taking the opportunity to broadcast his crimes himself he engaged in an alternative digital economy for which those early definitions of the snuff movie failed to account. This final chapter will explore this alternative economy and consider whether, in the twenty-first century and the era of participatory media, it is time to redefine the central tenets of what constitutes a snuff movie.

Understanding the Market that Exists for Real Murder

Images and videos of real death proliferate online and have done since the earliest days of the internet. Sue Tait has argued that digital technologies have transformed our access to documentary imagery of the dead and dying to such a large degree that 'the carnage that cinema imagined in the twentieth century is available online "for real" in the twenty-first' (2009: 334). While there are a variety of websites that might host images and videos of this kind, undoubtedly the most extreme examples of this material can be accessed via 'Shock Sites'. Often incorrectly labelled as 'snuff sites' in the press, in their simplest form 'Shock Sites' are websites that host content that is intended to be offensive and/or disturbing to its viewers. This material is often pornographic, scatological, racist, sexist, homophobic or graphically violent in nature, though, for a great many of these websites, much of this is often couched in humour.

The earliest 'Shock Sites' were not fully formed websites as we might understand them today but were instead often comprised of just one or two pages, often hosting only one image. Notable examples of this include *Goatse* (1999); a now infamous photo in which a naked man bent double stretches his anus open wide with both hands; *Tubgirl* (2001), an image routinely cited as one of the most disturbing on the internet, in which a young Japanese woman is lying in the bath with her legs in the air as she squirts an explosive orange enema from her anus onto her own face and; *Lemon Party* (2002), an image that depicts three naked elderly men who are engaged in an orgy, the first man fellating the second, who kisses the third man. These images belong to a discreet body of bait-and-switch pranks which were popular in the early 2000s and of which 'Rickrolling' is arguably the most well-known example. However, where 'Rickrolling' involved posting a hyperlink to a supposedly relevant topic, which then re-directed the viewer to the music video of Rick Astley's 1987 hit 'Never Gonna Give You Up', these bait-and-switch pranks redirect to extreme imagery, like those listed above. Susanna Paasonen suggests that imagery of this kind is designed to appeal to 'the affective registers of amusement and disgust' (2017: 3), and while this emphasis does not preclude a sexual response, it is important to understand that in this context, this is not the primary motivation for sharing.

Steve Jones has argued that images and films of this kind proliferate because they are seen to 'transgress normative boundaries' and often rely upon a dominant heteronormative culture that celebrates the female body as a locus of sexual attraction, while actively constructing the homosexualised male body as a site of comic disgust or amusement (2010: 128). This framing can certainly be seen with the *Goatse* and *Lemon Party* memes, and it is a trend that can be seen to culminate in the circulation of *Meatspin*, a short-looped clip taken from the transsexual adult film *TSBitches* (2004). The clip features a tightly framed shot of a man penetrating a transgender woman. The motion of intercourse has caused the transgender woman's penis to spin around. A spin counter counts up every time the penis spins and this is set to the theme of Dead or Alive's hit song 'You Spin Me Right Round (Like a Record)'. When the counter reaches forty-five spins, you are greeted by a text box that reads 'YOU ARE OFFICIALLY GAY :-)'. Memes like this are unquestionably reliant upon a performatively homophobic response to non-heteronormative practice, and Steve Jones has argued that images and videos of this kind, and the shock sites that host them, 'unabashedly work against an axis of normality' (2010: 129). Here 'obscene images are offensive because they contravene moral principles or because they portray what is considered to be indecent or repugnant' (2010: 123).

Arguably the most notorious viral video to mobilise ideas of what is indecent or repugnant is *2Girls1Cup*, a fetish video that is focussed on coprophagia and that features two women defecating into a cup and then taking turns to consume the excrement before then vomiting into each other's mouths. *2Girls1Cup* is the unofficial name given to the trailer for *Hungry Bitches*, a 2007 Brazilian scat fetish pornographic film. The video went viral, aided in no small part by the success of reaction videos that focussed explicitly on the faces of viewers as they endured the video's graphic content. Clearly, for those who accessed *2Girls1Cup*, the pleasure was not derived from their own individual scatological fetish, but from the experience of enduring the video, and then, for a large proportion of these viewers, the process of documenting their own affective responses in performative reaction videos that flooded the internet. Indeed, the video was so successful that it inspired a pseudo-genre of extreme content that each followed the same naming conventions as *2 Girls 1 Cup*. *2 Girls 1 Finger*, *8 Girls No Cup*, *1 Guy 1 Jar*, *1 Guy 1 Screwdriver*, *3 Orangutans 1 Blender*, and *1 Girl 1 Cake* were all notable examples of viral videos that followed this naming convention and that traded on a sense of shock and/or disgust that was often articulated through the transgression of heteronormative desire. However, and as Steve Jones has argued:

> Not all shock site imagery works against sexuality, age, or weight taboos so explicitly; Tubgirl, and the 'Hello.jpg' of Goatse may be partially informed by these discourses, but their ability to shock arises primarily from pushing the body beyond its expected limits (in the case of the latter, by stretching a distended anus to a remarkable degree). However, both use the same normative body-conception to Other bodies whose integrity has been compromised. (2010: 128-129)

A film that sits at this intersection is the 30-second viral porn video *2 Guys 1 Horse*, a video that shows a man being anally penetrated by a horse. Susanna Paasonen suggests that *2 Guys 1 Horse* is likely the most widely known instance of animal porn and attributes its notoriety to 'its status as a semi-snuff film', in which 'actual bodily harm is occurring' (2014: 208). Paasonen terms the film 'semi-snuff' because the internal injuries sustained during filming would result in the death of the performer, Washington resident, Kenneth Pinyan. However, in the context in which it was shared, the response to *2 Guys 1 Horse* was much the same as the response to *2 Girls 1 Cup*. Paasonen's work documents how reaction videos, in which viewers documented their own performatively visceral responses to the clip, became pivotal to the continued circulation of the film, noting that much like *Goatse* and *Lemon Party* before it, *2 Guys 1 Horse* was 'distributed as extreme and shock pornography with the intention to shock and disgust, rather than to sexually arouse' (2014: 208).

Discussion thus far has prioritised imagery that is broadly pornographic in nature, and that is because so much of this culture relies on ideas of sexual transgression to shock and offend. However, the distinction that Paasonen makes is fundamental to understanding the market that exists for extreme imagery that sits outside of the pornographic, and that is because it is arguably the same impulse that drives access to *this* material. The same performatively visceral reaction videos can be seen documenting responses to material that is more violent in nature, with the same emphasis given to humour articulated through shock and offense. Shock Sites host an array of material that sits outside of the pornographic or the scatological. This can range from footage of car accidents, war crimes, autopsies, suicides or even newsreel footage deemed too graphic for broadcast and, for the most part, these videos serve a similar function as *2Girls 1Cup*. They are videos that are presented in order to appeal to the affective registers of disgust and amusement. This is important because it is these same websites that are routinely labelled as 'snuff sites' in the press, a label that disguises much of the real motivation that most have for visiting them.

While not a 'genre' in the traditional sense, material on these websites sits at the intersection between horror, amusement and disgust, and responses to imagery and film of this kind are probably best understood through an appropriation of Philip Brophy's concept of 'Horrality'. Brophy suggested that 'the gratification of the contemporary horror film is based upon tension, fear, anxiety, sadism and masochism – a disposition that is overall both tasteless and morbid' (1986: 5). Using 'Horrality', Brophy described a trend in the contemporary horror film to combine elements of horror, textuality, morality, and hilarity, likening it to the effect of 'a death-defying carnival ride' (1986: 5). While the imagery that is hosted on Shock Sites is infinitely more extreme than anything that Brophy was describing, responses to films of this kind nevertheless articulate a familiar emphasis on horror, on textuality, on morality, and on hilarity.

While these sites all facilitate a morbid fascination with death, it is a mistake to understand engagement with this kind of material as an inherently deviant and sexually motivated activity. It is perhaps better understood as a largely gendered homosocial activity in which men perform their disgust and their humour in their ability to tolerate imagery that they consider difficult and challenging – a kind of 'extreme horrality'. While niche, these are not playing to the completely marginal communities that you might expect, with websites like Rotton.com, Ogrish.com, and Bestgore.com (all of which hosted videos and images of the dead and dying) routinely advertised in alternative 'lads' mag' *Bizarre*, which was available on any high street in the UK before ceasing publication in 2015. The videos and images that were showcased on these websites were often accompanied by humorous comments from a community of people who were invested in seeing the most extreme imagery available online, with a strange kind of badge of honour attached to having experienced the most extreme images that the internet had to offer.

However, while humorous responses to challenging material became a central part of these communities, there are examples where even the core membership was shaken by what they had seen. In 2007 a video that originated in Dnepropetrovsk (Ukraine's third-largest city, now Dnipro) and that followed the same naming conventions as those detailed above was uploaded to the Shock Sites Ogrish.com and theYNC.com. *3 Guys 1 Hammer* was a blurry eight-minute video that appeared to show two men using a hammer and a screwdriver to brutally murder an elderly man. It later transpired that the victim was Sergei Yatzenko, who was murdered in Dnepropetrovsk on the 12 July 2007. Bodies began appearing in the street and the people of Dnepropetrovsk were gripped by fear. The press named the killers the Dnepropetrovsk Maniacs, and a task force was set up to try and find them.

The killers were finally apprehended when they tried to sell a mobile phone belonging to one of their victims. At the trial, it was revealed that Igor Suprunyuk and Viktor Sayenko had begun by torturing and killing animals before progressing to women, children, and elderly men, often torturing and mutilating their bodies after bludgeoning their victims with a hammer. The court saw over 300 photos and two videos that documented their crimes in forensic detail. However, it was only after the pair had been in custody for a month that *3 Guys 1 Hammer* appeared online, apparently leaked by someone associated with the prosecution. Inevitably, speculation began to build that the videos and images had been produced to order for a collector of snuff movies (Anon, 2007), but this was quickly dismissed by the Regional security chief, Ivan Stupak, who stated categorically that there was no evidence to support this (Leontyeva 2007).

Bogdan Vlasenko, the main detective assigned to the case believed instead that 'they were doing it as a hobby, to have a collection of memories when they get old' (Anon, 2008). Nevertheless, Vlasenko's belief was largely ignored in coverage that widely reported the crimes of the Dnepropetrovsk Maniacs as 'proof' of snuff.

While the reaction videos that had by now become a staple of this pseudo genre inevitably appeared online, initial responses to the video were altogether more muted. In *Killing for Culture*, Kerekes and Slater document some of these and note that these were not the responses of perverse titillation, and that 'even among seasoned consumers of hardcore shocks', there was concern that they had just seen a real murder (all quotes below taken from Kerekes and Slater, 2016: 407-410).

OK, saw this 1 hour ago on another forum, it's still in my mind and I think it will be for a couple of days. Fuck, I thought I was desensitized. I'm not.

> ... Jeez. I didn't know what to do. Seriously. I just froze looking at it in slow motion. I was wishing with all I could that that man would no longer move, so it would stop, but they just kept going and going.

Another user who had previously sought out videos of beheadings from Jihadi terrorists and mangled accident victims said:

> ... I wanted to weep, but I couldn't. I was just broken inside. The images have haunted me for the last few days. Now I understand why people would want a 'grief counsellor' after some horrendous incident. I feel like I need a grief counsellor. This is a whole new level. I don't know what to say. I'm still in a daze. I'm a little disoriented. This is unbelievable.

While another said:

> ... I thought I was a cold-blooded motherfucker when it came to watching these gore videos, but this one really got to me; like staring into the face of true evil.

Kerekes and Slater suggest that although these quotations represent only a tiny fraction of the comments, the tone is largely representative of responses to the film, and while videos of beheadings might 'elicit some flippant or wholly dismissive remarks', responses to this film were altogether more sombre in tone, revealing much about the community.

Inevitably, users began speculating that what they had witnessed was the first legitimate snuff movie. However, a user calling himself Ultimax was quick to clarify:

> I hate to say it, but this is not a snuff video. A snuff video is a video made with the intention of making a profit off it. These assholes made this video as a trophy and to get off on later. However, if they made these videos and sold them to friends (or something like that), then that would be considered a snuff film. This is by far one of the closet [sic] you will get to a real snuff film though. There was one other instance like this with a serial killer, but his videos were for trophy as well. Either way, very sad.

And while this cannot be considered as snuff movie for all of the reasons stated above, a film that would present the first legitimate challenge to the myth of the snuff movie was about to emerge and would similarly shake up the internet.

CHALLENGING THE MYTH OF *SNUFF*

On December 22, 2010, a video was uploaded to YouTube entitled *1 Boy 2 Kittens*. The video appeared to show a teenage boy whose face was obscured putting two kittens into a plastic bag, sealing the bag and then sucking the air out with a vacuum cleaner. As the kittens died, he sang Christmas carols. As you might expect, reaction to the video was instantaneous, and although the video was quickly removed, it became a catalyst for animal rights activists who launched a campaign to find the killer. The community grew quickly with members in America, Australia, Great Britain and Canada, concerned that the killer was just developing an appetite for murder, and citing evidence that many of the world's most notorious serial killers – Ian Brady, Ed Kemper, Jeffrey Dahmer, Albert DeSalvo (the 'Boston Strangler') and David Berkowitz (the 'Son of Sam') – had all begun by killing animals. The community analysed the clip for any clue that might help identify the killer, and despite its limited runtime, they were able to derive much information from the video, but not enough to identify the perpetrator.

The group received an unsolicited message on Facebook from a user calling themselves Beverly Kent. The message read 'the name of the kitten vacummer [sic] you are looking for is Luka Magnotta' (Jenson, 2014). When the group searched for Magnotta they found hundreds of articles, images and videos, mostly user-generated material that presented Magnotta as a globe-trotting model. There were rumours that he was dating Michael Jackson and Madonna, and there was a video slideshow showing him modelling multiple outfits to New Order's 'True Faith' (1987). In 2007 *Toronto Sun* had interviewed Magnotta addressing rumours that he had dated the infamous Canadian murderess Karla Homolka (Jenson, 2014). The web was filled with fan pages and posts dedicated to Magnotta, from speculation about whether he and River Phoenix were cousins, to the suggestion that he had been arrested trying to enter Area 51.

It would later be revealed that all of this content was fake and generated by Magnotta, who maintained over seventy Facebook profiles and twenty personal websites (Parker, 2012). Magnotta craved attention, and on December 2, 2011, he uploaded another video, entitled *Python Christmas*, in which he fed a live kitten to a python to the tune of 'Little Drummer Boy'. Another appeared soon after, in which he duct-taped a kitten to a stick and then drowned it in the bathtub. The group worked out that the python video was uploaded from an account registered in Islington, and while it was initially believed that he was using a Virtual Private Network (VPN) to protect his location, a journalist from *The Sun* newspaper managed to track him down to a hotel in London. Magnotta denied all involvement and even threated to take legal action against the newspaper for harassment. But shortly afterwards, *The Sun* news desk received an email that read:

> Well, I have to say goodbye for now, but don't worry, in the near future you'll be hearing from me again. This time, however, the victims won't be small animals. I will, however, send you a copy of the new video I'm going to be making. You see, killing is different than smoking… with smoking you can actually quit. Once you kill and taste blood it's impossible to stop. The urge is just too strong not to continue. You have some very sexy journalists at your paper :) I have one I'm very keen on now. He was very sexy. You know, the fun part of all this is watching millions of people get angry and frustrated because they can't catch me. That's why I love this. I love the risk factor. It's so fun watching people work so hard gathering all the evidence, then not being able to name me or catch me. You see, I always win. I always hold the trump card and I will continue to make more movies. London is wonderful because all the people are so stupid. It's easy. So, I have to disappear for a while, you know… until people quit bothering me… but next time you hear from me it will be in a movie I am producing, that will have some humans in it, not just pussies :) The things I've seen and the things

I've done, you can only imagine... Well, it was fun fucking around with everyone, so have a merry Christmas and a happy new years. I know I will. :) Getting away with all this, now that's genius. (West, 2020).

The email was signed 'John Kilbride', a reference to the second victim of the Moors murderers, Ian Brady and Myra Hindley. It was also later revealed that Magnotta's use of 'Little Drummer Boy' was likely a reference to the murder of ten-year-old Lesley Ann Downey, another of Brady's and Hindley's victims, whose murder was recorded on audio cassette with the song playing in the background to drown out the sound of her screams.

Members of the group monitoring Magnotta managed to track him down to Montreal by piecing together shreds of evidence from his numerous online profiles and tried to enlist the help of the local police, but found them unsympathetic. Unaware of the letter to *The Sun*, Montreal police were unwilling to expend the resources it would take to track someone whose only crime at that time was killing cats. The group tried to impress upon the police the likelihood that Magnotta would progress to human victims, but their concerns went unheeded. On May 25, 2012, an 11-minute video entitled *1 Lunatic, 1 Ice Pick* was uploaded to the Shock Sites TheYNC and Best Gore. This video sent shockwaves around the internet. The film was recorded in a darkened room and featured the figure of a naked man tied to the frame of a bed in front of a poster of the film *Casablanca* (1942). The man is repeatedly stabbed, with his assailant plunging an ice pick (later revealed to be a screwdriver) into the body over and over again. He slices his throat, decapitates the body, and cuts off his legs and hand. He then guides the severed hand across his crotch, before sodomising the bloodied torso. He takes a knife and carves the flesh from the victim's buttocks, inviting a puppy to eat from the bloodied stumps of his legs. The corpse is then sodomized with a bottle, before the film closes with a series of snapshots of moments from the mutilation.

The video achieved notoriety overnight, and on one of the sites that still hosts the video, its preview alone has received 4,831,048 at the time of writing. While this illustrates an unprecedented level of interest in such a video, and many might argue that this is surely evidence of a depraved audience for snuff movies, as already detailed, these were not the imagined audience of deviants paying large sums of money to feed their perversion.

Instead, the film was shared as part of the same culture detailed above, with viewers documenting their own affective responses to the murder of Jun Lin in the same way that they had with *2 Girls 1 Cup*.

On the surface, *1 Lunatic 1 IcePick* does not conform to the FBI definition of what constitutes a snuff movie any more than *3 Guys 1 Hammer*. It did not circulate via some underground network. It was not produced for the sexual gratification of its audience. It did not change hands for increasingly large sums of money, and perhaps most importantly, Magnotta was not paid to produce the film. However, while Magnotta did not receive money for the production of the film, he did benefit from it, achieving a celebrity status that he coveted and that, for him, far exceeded monetary value.

CELEBRITY AND THE SERIAL KILLER

In his book, *Natural Born Celebrities: Serial Killers in American Culture* (2005), David Schmid explores the intersection between stardom and violence in contemporary America. He traces the emergence of the celebrity serial killer and observes that hegemonic definitions of fame tend to present it as an inherently positive phenomenon in which fame is achieved by the talented on a meritorious basis. However, he argues that 'the iconic status of serial killers in contemporary American culture' provides 'compelling evidence of the collapse in the difference between fame and notoriety', going on to suggest that all too often 'today the famous are often the visible, rather than the talented' (2005: 297). That visibility has always been dependent upon the mass media, and from Jack the Ripper to (allegedly) O. J. Simpson the celebrity status of killers has continued to be amplified by the media coverage that they receive for their crimes.

Charles Manson and 'the Manson family', whose crimes only amplified the myth of the snuff movie, are the prime example of the ways in which the lines between fame and infamy have become blurred. Manson himself achieved a kind of grotesque celebrity which, right up until his death in 2017, afforded him a legion of fans who followed him on his Twitter page, somewhat disturbingly, under the handle of Helter Skelter, a reference to the Tate/LaBianca murders for which he was imprisoned (Davis, 2009). Manson's celebrity status has even contributed to a booming market in what Andy

Kahan, the director of the Houston-based Mayor's Crime Victims Office, dubbed 'murderabilia' – the memorabilia of celebrity murderers (Hylton, 2007). Manson's prison art routinely sells for three- and four-figure prices, a lock of his hair and even his prison flip-flops were made available for sale, and all successfully found their way onto the market and into the hands of collectors who would pay increasingly large sums of money for objects associated with America's most notorious serial killer. However, Manson is by no means unique in this phenomenon. The license plate from John Wayne Gacy's snowplough sold for $1,700, and even a hand-addressed envelope from jailed Panamanian General Manuel Noriega sold for $350. This online interest has not only provided a platform for celebrity killers, but it has also provided a platform to those who would *be* celebrity killers.

Luka Magnotta was desperate to be famous. Born Eric Newman in Ontario in 1982, he had tried and failed on numerous occasions to become a successful model and television star. When this failed, he used the internet to share his crimes and then revelled in the attention and notoriety that this afforded him. Magnotta was obsessed with celebrity. In 2005 he appeared as a pin-up model, under the pseudonym 'Jimmy', then the following year, he changed his name to Luka Magnotta and began developing his persona. Following a short-lived career as a gay porn star and finding occasional work as a stripper and a male escort, he auditioned for OUTtv's reality series *COVERguy* but was ultimately rejected. It was around this time that stories began to emerge that Magnotta was in a relationship with the serial killer Karla Homolka. He was interviewed for *Toronto's Sun* and denied having any association with Homolka, arguing that these rumours were ruining his career.

Latterly, it would become clear that Magnotta himself was the source of this misinformation and that he was attempting to elevate his own star status by capitalising on the visibility of Homolka's recent high-profile release. By 2008, Magnotta had undergone multiple cosmetic surgery procedures and auditioned for the Slice network show *Plastic Makes Perfect*, but again was unsuccessful. Unable to achieve the success that he desired in his everyday life, he began building a complex network of identities and personas online. He developed at least seventy Facebook profiles that interacted with each other and that cross-referenced information that he posted on discussion forums, on websites and blogs. These personas worked together to construct a narrative that presented him as an important figure linked to killers and celebrities. He created multiple channels on YouTube that purported to be fan channels dedicated to him, each posting videos that celebrated Magnotta as the 'sexiest man alive' (tigertigerburning4, 2008). Some of these avatars, known as 'sock puppets', were barely developed identities that played only a supporting role in the broader narrative, while others were far more established, with friends numbering in the hundreds and thousands, all developed with the sole intention of promoting Magnotta's celebrity. He doctored photographs to make it seem as if he was successful and popular, placing himself in exotic locations, in expensive cars, relaxing with friends, and even as the groom at his own wedding. He linked himself to celebrities like Marilyn Monroe, James Dean, John Lennon, Michael Jackson, and Madonna, and, in the case of the latter, suggested through one of his 'sock puppet' accounts that 'she is dating Luka Magnotta just so you know' (D'aliesio and Freeze, 2012). He was fascinated by the Russian mafia, often claiming to be from Russia originally, and through his alias Vladimir Romanovs (a reference to a Soviet-Russian serial killer, rapist and paedophile), he would post images of the Russian mob and videos of people being killed in Russia. Over a period of years, Magnotta built up myriad identities to present fictitious information about himself, information that he would later dismiss as being part of an elaborate campaign to muddy his good name. In this way, he could maintain the illusion that he was a celebrity who was tired of the constant attention while working behind the scenes to direct that attention toward himself.

1 Boy 2 Kittens was initially uploaded to the YouTube channel Uonlywish500 on December 21, 2010, a channel which had only one comment: 'All haters can suck my huge dick ,,, LOL.' When the video was removed, all that was left was a link to a video from the film *Catch Me if You Can* (2002), a taunt to anyone who would try to find him. As more videos appeared online, the Facebook group dedicated to finding him doubled their efforts and began cross-referencing Facebook accounts, Flickr accounts, and Dailymotion videos. They examined the metadata on images posted to the internet and began trying to triangulate Magnotta's location, matching locales from his images to locations found on GoogleMaps. It soon became evident that Magnotta lived in a fantasy world in which he was a famous model and bisexual porn star. They found numerous articles, written by Magnotta himself, typically in the third person, presented as the work of a fan or a reporter who was obsessed with him. It was clear Magnotta was relishing the attention he was receiving from his videos *1 Boy 2 Kittens*, *Python Christmas* and *Bath Time LOL*, and shortly afterwards he began developing the plan to murder Lin Jun in the production of *1 Lunatic, 1 Ice Pick*.

Magnotta was a failed model, stripper, porn star and television star who craved attention. The internet afforded him a space in which he could cultivate a brand, directing interest to himself through his fictitious associations with Karla Homolka and Madonna. Tragically, in the murder of Lin Jun, Magnotta demonstrates perfectly David Schmid's belief that the differences between fame and notoriety have collapsed and that 'today the famous are often the visible, rather than the talented' (2015: 297). In 2019, Magnotta was the subject of a Netflix documentary *Don't F**k With Cats: Hunting an Internet Killer*, and he will forever be remembered as a killer who raped, butchered and even ate parts of his victim. While Magnotta did not receive any financial remuneration from the production of these videos, that is not to say that he did not profit from them. He achieved his goal: celebrity.

SNUFF IN AN ATTENTION ECONOMY

Michael H. Goldhaber has argued that since we are increasingly living our lives on the World Wide Web, not only do the economic laws that govern these spaces need to be appropriate to this new world, but that they also differ greatly from the principles established through traditional economics. Goldhaber suggests that this move online has seen society move from rubrics established under 'the information age', toward an economy based upon attention. He argues that this 'attention economy' brings with it its own kind of wealth, its own class divisions and its own forms of property, all of which make it incompatible with the industrial-money-market based economy it bids to replace. He concludes that 'success will come to those who best accommodate to this new reality' (1997).

This concept of the attention economy is vitally important not only in understanding Magnotta's motivations but also if we are to understand the motivation of viewers of the kind of extreme media discussed throughout this book. The web is filled with ordinary people documenting their performative responses to incredibly challenging imagery, and alongside those couched in performatively homophobic responses to non-heteronormative practices, many are documenting their affective responses to imagery of death and murder. In this new economy, Goldhaber makes a distinction between stars and fans, but increasingly, and as we have already seen, the shift that has democratised the means of production has made stars and producers of fans who are eager to document their own visceral reactions to extreme media online. These videos are then hosted on their own branded channels on YouTube or Vimeo, and reactions are broadcast across social media. Yeran Kim has argued that reaction videos, such as those discussed, 'have a formative effect on the attention economy by means of shifting attention from the … stars … to ordinary people' (2015: 334), and while Kim's research is primarily concerned with reactions to the music videos of K-Pop stars, there is a continuity here that is worth considering. What is perhaps most significant in the reaction videos to *1 Lunatic 1 Icepick*, is that ultimately, and in spite of his notoriety, Magnotta himself plays only a peripheral role, second to both the crimes he committed, and to the reactions of those watching.

Nevertheless, the question remains, whether Magnotta's fascination with, and eventual elevation to, celebrity, is enough to constitute profit, and thereby facilitate a shift in the established definition of the snuff movie. In many ways, Magnotta can be understood as a micro-celebrity, which Theresa Senft has defined as a 'new style of online performance that involves people "amping up" their popularity over the Web using technologies like video, blogs and social networking sites' (2008: 25). Magnotta's quest for fame saw him do exactly that, spreading stories about his popularity and his success across the web, through videos, blogs and social networking sites. But when these stories failed to generate the kind of attention that he desired, Magnotta began killing cats, before moving on to the murder of Lin Jun. Magnotta did not appear to care about money; that was not a motivating factor here. He cared about celebrity, to such a degree that when he was apprehended, he was caught in an internet café searching online for himself.

While snuff has always had a precise definition, discursively, for many, it has simply become shorthand for any film that depicts images of real murder. From that perspective, *1 Lunatic 1 Icepick* is unequivocally a snuff movie; but if we accept this kind of terminological fluidity, then we open the door to any film that features imagery of a real murder happening on camera, being classified as snuff – from images of the holocaust to the assassination of John F. Kennedy, from footage of 9/11 to beheadings in the Middle East. While language has a way of evolving, I would argue that the term 'snuff' would lose all meaning if we were to begin categorising any film that included imagery of real death as proof of the existence of the snuff movie. But if we redefine what we mean by 'profit', then the case of Luka Magnotta may indeed be the first legitimate snuff movie.

Conclusion

This book has attempted to map the many ways that the cultural mythology of the snuff movie is reliant on ideas and iconography that were a core part of Allan Shackleton's coda to *Snuff*, and to demonstrate how these narratives often still trade on the specifics of that sequence. This is not a straightforward narrative, but it is a narrative that has demonstrably reworked that hyperbolic conclusion of Shackleton's *Snuff* as rumour, with the same elements occurring in multiple accounts and in a variety of contexts across the United Kingdom and the United States. From the early accounts of prominent feminist activist Catherine Risingflame Moirai to the account of the American radical feminist Andrea Dworkin, from Irish campaigner Clodagh Corcoran to the papers of Mary Whitehouse and the National Viewers' and Listeners' Association (NVLA), right up to the present day and the account of the radical feminist writer Julie Bindel – there is a line that can be traced that leads back to the fictional film, *Snuff*. It is a narrative that has been repeated over and over again in accounts that often appear to be referencing the film *Snuff* rather than anything approaching an actual snuff movie. It is a myth that arguably begins with the rumours circulated by the Campaign for Decency, but it is an idea that has been reworked and revised as it reverberated through popular culture. Polly Toynbee's account in *The Guardian* discussed in Chapter 4 is just one such account, and while patently not true, these accounts have been repeated over and over again, and risk being given more credence each time they are repeated.

In its original form it is a narrative that is deeply indebted to 'the Manson Family' murders and the belief that footage exists that documents in gory detail the brutality of their crimes. This connection was only reinforced when Shackleton took the decision to use the Findlays film *The Slaughter* (with its faux Manson gang) as the basis of his snuff movie. In doing so, Shackleton forever tied 'the Manson Family' murders to the idea of the snuff movie and the continued dependence on Manson as a core aspect of snuff narratives can be seen in the documents from the NVLA Archive and the belief that real snuff movies were being produced in California by 'the Family'. This is a narrative that relies heavily on the Othering of other cultures. As already evidenced, in North America, the threat of snuff came from South America; in the United Kingdom, the threat of snuff came from Amsterdam or California; and contemporary accounts often insist that snuff originates in Eastern Europe, Cambodia or the Philippines, a perception no doubt drawn from the trade in sex tourism that too often centres on children. This is the cultural legacy of *Snuff* in an Anglo/American context, a blurring between reality and fiction in which the possibility that snuff might exist has become the only evidence needed for proof of its existence. In South America, at least for those who are aware, the film has very different connotations and a legacy that can be seen to capitalise on 'the missing' and 'the disappeared' of 'the Dirty War'. In this context, Shackleton's hyperbolic come-on that the 'film that could only be made in South America where life is cheap' is not simply an exploitative or titillating tagline, but instead a starkly flippant reminder of a tragic period in the country's history.

Reminders of 'the Dirty War' are still all around and traces of *Snuff*'s central conceit can be seen in much of this media coverage. In 2008, Mario Oscar 'El Malevo' Ferreyra, a former police chief and an officer during the National Reorganisation Process, climbed a water tower in an attempt to evade arrest. He had been responsible for the murders of thousands, and as the police closed in and he realised that he had no means of escape, he said simply 'I say goodbye' (in translation) and shot himself in the head. His death was filmed at point-blank range and broadcast live on national television (Elsinger, 2008). Similarly, in 1981 the magazine *Gente* was prosecuted for publishing post-mortem photographs of the Argentine lawyer and politician Ricardo Balbín. Balbín had been an early opponent of the military coup but was later denounced for not opposing the atrocities of 'the Dirty War'. He died in 1981 and photos of his dead body appeared in the press shortly after, though his family contested the publication and went on to win a tribunal against the magazine. Outside of the political sphere, in 2019, Argentinian news outlets were criticised for printing pictures and broadcasting videos of the lifeless naked body of the model Natacha Jaitt (Anon, 2019), while in 2012, the newspaper *Crónica* was prosecuted for publishing the leaked photographs of the body of model Jasmín De Grazia as a magazine supplement under the headline 'Poor Jazmin'.

Reports like this are by no means unique to Argentina, but they do raise important questions about the motivation to broadcast and publish imagery of this kind, particularly in the format of a glossy magazine such as *Crónica*'s supplementary issue. In her exploration of the reading protocols that surround celebrity gossip magazines, Andrea McDonnell suggests that when 'confronted with an endless parade of exceptionally thin, gorgeous, and wealthy celebs, readers express their frustration at these unrealistic "norms"', going on to argue that magazines much like *Crónica* are designed to encourage this kind of reading, a reading that casts the audience as 'adjudicators in their moral universe' (2014). McDonnell suggests that schadenfreude is a fundamental aspect of engagement in celebrity gossip magazine culture and cites photo editor Susanne Reith's belief that stories that illustrate negative elements of fame are among the most popular in their readership, and that readers 'use tales of celebrity failure as a way of temporarily block out their [own] troubles' (2014). It is possible that the publication of images like those of Jasmine De Grazia are an extension of this kind of reading protocol; however, in a magazine culture that oscillates between celebrating the beauty and sexuality of their subjects one week, to dismissing them over unflattering bikini shots the next, articles like this, in magazines like *Crónica*, risk sexualising the naked body of the dead model. By publishing and profiting from reproducing these images the magazine may have fulfilled both sexual and commercial criteria of the snuff movie and while it is unlikely that any of these cases would legitimately be categorised as snuff, each demonstrates how accustomed we are becoming to exposure to extreme imagery, and how this imagery is often packaged as entertainment. Arguably, the market that exists for *I Lunatic I Icepick* is simply an extension of these reading protocols, and while I have argued that the film could be read as the first legitimate snuff movie, the increased visibility of reporting of this kind suggests that perhaps we should no longer be looking to the world of marginal exploitation cinema or the Dark Web for examples of snuff, but that images and films of death and murder have been subsumed into mainstream entertainment culture.

Bibliography

Abel, Bob (1975) 'Roberta Findlay: She's No Angel'. *Film International Magazine*, Volume 1, Number 2, May.

Acland, Charles R. (ed.) (2006) *Residual Media: Residual Technologies and Culture*. Minneapolis: University of Minnesota Press.

Allard, Andy (2010) 'SNUFF Blue Sleeve'. Pre-cert.co.uk. Available at: www.pre-cert.co.uk/forum/showthread.php?t=16562

Anon (1960) 'Vulgar, Pointless, in Bad Taste But Mr Teas Not Pornography'. *Variety*, Nov 2, 1960, pg. 46.

Anon (1975) 'Doubt actual kill in Manson-angled porno-murder pic'. *Variety*, Oct 8, 1975, pg. 1.

Anon (1975a) 'Argentine Snuff to US'. *The Independent Film Journal*. Nov 26, 1975; 76, 13; pg. 15.

Anon (1975b) 'Snuff (Sex Murders) Film Now Thought Hoax from Argentina'. *Variety*. Dec 17, 281, 6; pg. 4.

Anon (1975c) 'Snuff World Premiere Is Set for Indy in January'. *Boxoffice*. Dec 22, 108, 11/12; pg. 11.

Anon (1975d) 'Doubt actual kill in Manson-angled porno-murder pic'. *Variety* Oct 8, 280, 9; Entertainment Industry Magazine Archive pg. 1.

Anon (1976a) 'Victim in Snuff Says She Prefers Anonymity'. *Boxoffice*. Mar 22, 108, 24; pg. ME4.

Anon (1976b) 'Snuff Premieres in Indy'. *Boxoffice*. Feb 9, 1976; 108, 18; pg. C1.

Anon (1976c) 'Customs Approves 'Snuff' For U.S. Distribution'. *Boxoffice*. Jan 12, 1976; 108, 14; pg. 3.

Anon (1976d) 'Snuff Protested in Philly'. *Boxoffice*. Feb 23, 108, 20; pg. SE4.

Anon (1976e) 'Snuff Shown in Wichita; Violence Labeled "Fake"'. *Boxoffice*. Feb 9, 108, 18; pg. C-4.

Anon (1976f) 'Snuff Unreels in Vegas Subject To Many Limits'. *Variety*. Feb 25; 282, 3; pg. 36.

Anon (1976g) 'Film Reviews: Snuff'. *Variety*. Feb 25; 282, 3; pg. 22.

Anon (1977) 'Pictures Grosses: "Farmer" Happy $40,000, Cleve.; "Do It" Plush 42½G, "Show" 14G'. *Variety*, Los Angeles Vol. 286, Iss. 11.

Anon (n.d.) Clippings file, Archives of the National Viewers and Listeners Association, Albert Sloman Library, University of Essex.

Anon (1982a) 'Protests expected over Astra release of US "snuff" movie'. *Video Business*. June.

Anon (1982b) 'Snuff'. *Video Business*. Mid–June, Volume 2 Number 9, pg. 4.

Anon (1982c) 'Wall-To-Wall Gore'. *Video Business*, June pg. 27.

Anon (1982d) 'Snuff snuffs it'. *Television and Video Retailer*. June pg. 24.

Anon (1982) 'The Wizard from LA'. *Television and Video Retailer*. June pg. 52.

Anon (1983) 'Tougher times on the way for video nasty distributors'. *Video Viewer* 2, number 8. pg. 8

Anon (2007) '40 people ordered Dnepropetrovsk killers via the Internet'. *Rus.newsru. ua*. Available at: http://rus.newsru.ua/crime/30jul2007/ybijstva.html (accessed: 30 January 2020).

Anon (2008) 'Killing for Kicks – Youths Confess to 21 Murders'. *Russia Today*. Available at: http://www.russiatoday.com/news/news/23537 (accessed: 30 January 2020).

Anon (2012) 'Scandal about the photos of Jasmine de Grazia'. *Minutouno.com*. Available at: https://www.minutouno.com/notas/159889-escandalo-las-fotos-jazmin-grazia (accessed: 30 January 2020).

Anon (2019) 'Photos and video: so they found Natacha Jaitt's naked body'. *Nuevodiarioweb.com.ar*. Available at: http://www.nuevodiarioweb.com.ar/noticias/2019/02/23/185688-fotos-y-video-asi-encontraron-el-cuerpo-desnudo-de-natacha-jaitt (accessed: 30 January 2020).

Aras, Joaquin (2015) '1976 Snuff Video installation – Sound remake of the film Snuff'. *Joaquinaras.com*. Available at: http://joaquinaras.com.ar/index.php?/obras/snuff-1976/ (accessed: 20 September 2019).

Aras, Joaquin (2019) 'Joaquín Aras Mixdown'. *Soundcloud.com*. Available at: https://soundcloud.com/user-766042506/joaquin-aras-mixdown#t=0:00 (accessed: 20 September 2019).

Aras, Joaquin (2019) 'Overview'. Grand-union. Available at: https://grand-union.org.uk/events/screening-of-snuff-1976-qa-with-joaquin-aras-at-the-electric-cinema (accessed: 30 January 2022).

Aras, Joaquin (2020) Email to Mark McKenna, 2 January.

Belk, R. (2001) *Collecting in a Consumer Society*. London: Routledge.

Bindel, Julie (2006) 'The legacy of Jane Longhurst'. *The Guardian*. Available at: https://www.theguardian.com/uk/2006/sep/01/ukcrime.gender (accessed: 30 January 2022).

Bindel, Julie (2018) 'I've seen the type of violent snuff porn Peter Madsen viewed before he murdered Kim Wall – anyone who denies a connection is deluded'. *The Independent*. Available at: https://www.independent.co.uk/voices/kim-wall-peter-madsen-snuff-porn-submarine-inventor-submarine-swedish-journalist-a8322076.html (accessed: 19 September 2021).

Blumenthal, Ralph (1973) '"Hard-core" grows fashionable—and very profitable'. *New York Times*. January 21, pg. 28.

Brass, Dick (1975a) 'Snuff Porn? The Actress is Actually Killed'. *New York Post*. 1 October. 3, 15.

Brass, Dick (1975b) 'Peep Porn $$ Titillate Mob'. *New York Post*. 15 October. 3.

Brewster, Francis, Fenton, Harvey and Morris, Marc (2005) *Shock! Horror!: Astounding Artwork from the Video Nasty Era*. London: Fab Press.

Bronstein, Carolyn (2011) *Battling Pornography: The American Feminist Anti-Pornography Movement, 1976–1986*. Cambridge University Press: Cambridge.

Brownmiller, Susan (1999) *In Our Time: Memoir of a Revolution*. Dial Press: New York.

Philip Brophy (1986) 'Horrality – The Textuality of Contemporary Horror Films', *Screen*, Volume 27, Issue 1, January/February, Pages 2–13, https://doi.org/10.1093/screen/27.1.2.

Blakeley, Ruth (2009) *State Terrorism and Neoliberalism: The North in the South*. Routledge: Philadelphia.

Carol, Avedon (1993) 'Snuff: Believing in the Worst', in Alison Lassiter and Avedon Carol (eds) *Bad Girls and Dirty Pictures: The Challenge to Reclaim Feminism*. London: Pluto, pp. 126-130.

Chippendale, Peter (1982) 'How high street horror is invading the home', *The Sunday Times*. 23 May.

Chippendale, Peter (1982b) '"Nasty" squad jumps in on hunt for pirates', *The Sunday Times*, 12 Sept.

Cocchi, John (1976) 'Monarch Releasing Is Changing Its Image'. Entertainment Industry Magazine Archive, Dec 8, 1975; 108, 9; pg. 11.

Corcoran, Clodagh (1989) *Pornography: The New Terrorism*. Dublin: Attic Press.

D'aliesio, Renata and Freeze, Colin (2012) 'Body-parts suspect has a long Internet trail', *The Globe and Mail*. Available at: https://www.theglobeandmail.com/news/national/body-parts-suspect-has-a-long-internet-trail/article4219754/ (accessed: 30 January 2022).

Davis, Ivor (2009) 'The Devil's disciples: 40 years after his killing sprees, Charles Manson is now a grotesque celebrity with a Twitter page'. *The Daily Mail*. Available at: https://www.dailymail.co.uk/femail/article-1205141/The-Devils-disciples-40-years-killing-sprees-Charles-Manson-grotesque-celebrity-Twitter-page.html (accessed: October 2019).

Dawe, Tony (1982) 'This poison being peddled as home entertainment', *The Daily Express*. 28 May, pg. 7.

Dworkin, Andrea (1981) *Pornography: Men Possessing Women*. The Women's Press Ltd: London.

Eder, Richard (1976) '"Snuff" Is Pure Poison'. *New York Times*, March 7. Available at: https://www.nytimes.com/1976/03/07/archives/snuff-is-pure-poison-poison-snuff.html (accessed: 21 June 2019).

Edelstein, David (2006) 'Now Playing at Your Local Multiplex: Torture Porn'. *New York Magazine*. Available at: https://nymag.com/movies/features/15622 (accessed: 30 January 2022).

Egan, K. (2007) *Trash or Treasure: Censorship and the Changing Meanings of the Video Nasties*. Manchester: Manchester University Press.

Elsinger, Rubén (2008) 'Se suicidó el "Malevo" Ferreyra, símbolo de la represión en

Tucumán', *Clarín*, Buenos Aires, 21 November.

Feitlowitz, Marguerite (2011) *A Lexicon of Terror: Argentina and the Legacies of Torture*. Oxford University Press: Oxford.

Freedman, Estelle B. and D'Emilio, John (2012) *Intimate Matters: A History of Sexuality in America*. University of Chicago Press: Chicago.

Goldhaber, M. (1997) 'The attention economy and the net', *First Monday*, 2(4). Available at: http://firstmonday.org/ojs/index.php/fm/article/view/519/440 (accessed: 27 October 2019).

Glyn-Jones, Ann (1996) *Holding Up a Mirror: How Civilizations Decline*. Exeter: Imprint Academic.

Groves, Adam (n.d.) 'Snuff'. *The Bedlam Files*. Available at: https://thebedlamfiles.com/film/snuff (accessed: 30 January 2022).

Hagin, Boaz (2010) 'Killed Because of Lousy Ratings: The Hollywood History of Snuff', *Journal of Popular Film and Television*, 38:1, 44-51, DOI: 10.1080/01956050903578414

Hebditch, Dick and Anning, Nick (1988) *Porn Gold: Inside the Pornography Business*. London: Faber & Faber.

Heller-Nicholas, Alexandra (2009) 'Snuff Boxing: Revisiting the Snuff Coda', *Cinephile: The University of British Columbia's Film Journal*: Vancouver.

Heller-Nicholas, Alexandra (2014) *Found Footage Horror Films: Fear and the Appearance of Reality*. Jefferson, NC: McFarland.

Hellochas (2013) 'Now then, now then, now then: SNUFF Astra video poster'. *Pre-cert.co.uk*. Available at: http://www.pre-cert.co.uk/forum/showthread.php?t=40761& (accessed: 31 October 2013).

Hellochas (2010) SNUFF Blue Sleeve. *Pre-cert.co.uk*. Available at: http://www.pre-cert.co.uk/forum/showthread.php?t=16562 (accessed: 7 February 2014).

Hylton, Hilary (2007) 'Cracking Down on "Murderabilia"'. *Time.com*. Available at: http://content.time.com/time/nation/article/0,8599,1629655,00.html (accessed: October 2019).

Itzen, Catherine (1988) 'Sex and Censorship: the political implications' in Chester, Gail and Dickey, Julienne (eds) *Feminism and Censorship*. London: Prism.

Inglis, Sam (2018) 'Banned! Snuff (1971/76)', *The London Economic*. Available at: https://www.thelondoneconomic.com/film/banned-snuff-1971-76/09/09/ (accessed: 30 January 2020).

Jackson, N. (2003) 'The cultural construction of snuff', *Kinoeye*, Vol 3, Issue 5, 10 May.

Jackson, N. (2017) 'Forced Entry (Shaun Costello, 1972)'. *Porn Studies*, 4(3), 296–304. DOI:10.1080/23268743.2017.1333021

Jackson, Neil, Kimber, Shaun, Walker, Johnny and Watson, Thomas Joseph (2016) *Snuff: Real Death and Screen Media*. Bloomsbury: London.

Jacobson, Harlan (1976) 'If Snuff Killings Are Real, Film Violence Faces New Test'. *Variety* Dec 10, 281, 5; pg. 4.

Jenson, Bill (2014) 'Animal Instinct: How Cat-Loving Sleuths Found an Accused Killer Sadist'. *Rolling Stone.com*. Available at: https://www.rollingstone.com/culture/culture-news/animal-instinct-how-cat-loving-sleuths-found-an-accused-killer-sadist-111273/ (accessed: 21 October 2019).

Johnson, Eithne and Schaefer, Eric (1993) 'Soft Core/Hard Gore: Snuff as a Crisis in Meaning', in *Journal of Film and Video*, University of Illinois Press, (Volume 45, Numbers 2-3, Summer-Fall): pp. 40–59.

Jones, Mark and Carlin, Gerry (2016) 'Unfound Footage and Unfounded Rumours the Manson Family Murders and the Persistence of Snuff', in Jackson, Neil et al. (eds) *Snuff: Real Death and Screen Media*. London: Bloomsbury.

Jones, Steve (2010) 'Horrorporn/Pornhorror: The Problematic Communities and Contexts of Extreme Online Imagery', in Attwood, Feona (ed.) *Porn.com: making sense of online pornography*. Switzerland: Peter Lang.

Jones, S. (2011) 'Dying to be Seen: Snuff-Fiction's Problematic Fantasies of "Reality"'. *Scope*, 19, pp. 1-22.

Jones, Steve (2016) 'A View to a Kill: Perspectives of Faux-Snuff and Self', in Jackson, Neil et al. (eds) *Snuff: Real Death and Screen Media*. London: Bloomsbury. pp. 277–292.

Jones, Steve (2013) *Torture Porn: Popular Horror after Saw*. London: Palgrave Macmillan.

Jones, Steve and Mowlabocus, Sharif (2009) 'Hard Times and Rough Rides: The Legal and Ethical Impossibilities of Researching "Shock" Pornographies'. *Sexualities* 12 (5):613–628.

Kaitlyn, Tiffany (2020) 'The Secret Internet of TERFs', *The Atlantic*. Available at: https://www.theatlantic.com/technology/archive/2020/12/reddit-ovarit-the-donald/617320 (accessed: February 2022).

Kaminsky, Ralph (1976) 'AFAA Pickets "Snuff" Bow; New Rating Label Urged'. *Boxoffce*, Mar 22, 108, 24; pg. 9.

Kerekes, David & Slater, David (1994). *Killing for Culture*. Manchester: Creation Books.

Kerekes, David & Slater, David (2016a) *Killing for Culture: From Edison to Isis: A New History of Death on Film*. Manchester: Headpress.

Kerekes, David (2016b) 'A Culture of Change: Forward', in Jackson, Neil. et al. (eds) *Snuff: Real Death and Screen Media*. London: Bloomsbury. pp. ix-xvi

Kim, Yeran (2015) 'Globalization of the privatized self-image: the reaction video and its attention economy on YouTube', in Hjorth, Larissa and Khoo, Olivia (eds) *Routledge Handbook of New Media in Asia*. London: Routledge. pp. 333-342.

Kimber, Shaun (2014) 'Transgressive edge play and Srpski Film/A Serbian Film', *Horror Studies*, Volume 5, Number 1, April, pp. 107-125(19).

Leontyeva, Anna (2007) 'Why the "Dnieper maniacs" were killed: the main versions'. *Segodnya.ua*. Available at: https://www.segodnya.ua/ukraine/pochemu-ubivali-dneprovckie-manjaki-hlavnye-vercii-64769.html (accessed: 8 October 2019).

Lewis, Jon (2000) *Hollywood V. Hardcore: How the Struggle Over Censorship Created the Modern Film Industry*. New York: New York University Press.

Lyons, Charles (1997) *The New Censors: Movies and the Culture Wars*. Philadelphia: Temple University Press.

Lyons, Kevin (2019) 'Snuff (1976)', *eofftvreview.wordpress.com*. Available at: https://eofftvreview.wordpress.com/2019/01/13/snuff-1976/ (accessed: 30 January 2020).

McKenna, Mark (2020) *Nasty Business: The Marketing and Distribution of the Video Nasties*. Edinburgh: Edinburgh University Press.

Malm, Sara (2018) 'Danish inventor searched internet for 'beheaded girl agony' just hours before 'killing a journalist on his submarine' and dismembering her'. *Mail Online*, 9

March. Available at: https://www.dailymail.co.uk/news/article-5481331/Inventor-searched-beheaded-girl-agony-killing-journalist.html (accessed: September 20 2019).

McDonnell, Andrea (2014) *Reading Celebrity Gossip Magazines*. Cambridge: Polity.

Meyer, Bernard S., Bergan, Francis, Agata, Burton C., Agata, Seth H. (2006) *The History of the New York Court of Appeals: 1932-2003*. New York: Columbia University Press.

Miles, Tim (1983) 'Sadism for Six Year Olds'. *The Daily Mail*, pp. 1-2.

Milligan, Stephen (2015) *The Bloodiest Thing That Ever Happened in Front of a Camera*, Manchester: Headpress.

Nolte, David (c1987) 'The Queen of Exploitation'. *Crimson Celluloid*. Self published: Victoria, Australia.

Nowell, Richard (2011: 17) *Blood Money: A History of the First Teen Slasher Cycle*. New York: Continuum.

Orange, Richard (2017) "Danish submarine owner claims journalist Kim Wall died when she was hit by hatch cover". *The Telegraph*, 5 September. Available at: https://www.telegraph.co.uk/news/2017/09/05/danish-submarine-owner-claims-journalist-kim-wall-died-hit-hatch/ (accessed: 5 September 2017).

Orange, Richard (2018). "Peter Madsen sentenced to life for murdering journalist Kim Wall". *The Guardian*, 25 April. Available at: https://www.theguardian.com/world/2018/apr/25/peter-madsen-sentenced-life-murdering-kim-wall-submarine (accessed: 25 April 2018).

Paasonen, Susanna (2014) 'The Beast Within Materiality, Ethics and Animal Porn', in Attwood, F., Campbell, V., Hunter, I., Lockyer, S. (eds) *Controversial Images: Media Representations on the Edge*. London: Palgrave Macmillan.

Paasonen, Susanna (2017) 'Time to celebrate the most disgusting video online'. *Porn Studies* Vol. 4, no. 4: pp. 463-467.

Parker, Alan (2012) 'Are you Luka Rocco Magnotta's Facebook friend?' *Macleans.ca*. Available at: https://www.macleans.ca/politics/are-you-luka-magnottas-facebook-friend/ (accessed: October 21 2019).

Peary, Gerald (1978) 'Woman in Porn'. *Take One*. September, pp. 28-32.

Petley, Julian (2000) '"Snuffed Out": Nightmares in a Trading Standards Officer's Brain', in Mendik, Xavier and Harper, Graeme (eds) *Unruly Pleasures: The Cult Film and its Critics*. London: FAB Press.

Petley, J. (2005). 'Cannibal Holocaust and the Pornography of Death', in King, Geoff (ed.) *The Spectacle of the Real: From Hollywood to Reality TV and Beyond*. Chicago: University of Chicago Press.

Petley, J. (2016) 'The Way to Digital Death', in Jackson, Neil et al. (eds) *Snuff: Real Death and Screen Media*. London: Bloomsbury. pp. 23–46.

Proctor, William (2018) 'Cult Conversations: A Series on Horror, Exploitation and the Gothic'. *Confessions of an Aca-Fan*. Available at: http://henryjenkins.org/blog/2018/10/30/cult-conversations-a-series-on-horror-exploitation-and-the-gothic (accessed: 30 January 2022).

Randall, R. S. (1968) *Censorship of the movies: The social and political control of a mass medium*. Madison: University of Wisconsin Press.

Romero, Luis Alberto (2002) *A History of Argentina in the Twentieth Century*. Philadelphia: Pennsylvania State University Press.

Sanders, Ed (1972) *The Family: The Story of Charles Manson s Dune Buggy Attack* Battalion. London: Panther.

Schmid, David (2005) *Natural Born Celebrities: Serial Killers in American Culture*. Chicago: University of Chicago Press.

Senft, Theresa (2008). *Camgirls: Celebrity and Community in the Age of Social Networks*. New York: Peter Lang Publishing.

Smith, Anna Marie (1993) 'What is Pornography?': An Analysis of the Policy Statement of the Campaign against Pornography and Censorship. *Feminist Review*. Vol 43, Issue 1.

Smith, Clarissa (2016) 'Breathing New Life into Old Fears: Extreme Pornography and the Wider Politics of Snuff', in Jackson, Neil et al. (eds) *Snuff: Real Death and Screen Media*. London: Bloomsbury.

Stine, Scott Aaron (1999) 'The Snuff Film: The Making Of An Urban Legend', *Skeptical Inquirer*, Volume 23, No. 3.

Tait, Sue (2009) 'Visualising Technologies and the Ethics and Aesthetics of Screening

Death'. *Science as Culture*. Volume 18, 2009 - Issue 3: Techno-Death: Technology, Death and the Cultural Imagination.

Thompson, Bill (1994) *Soft Core: Battle Over Pornography in Britain and America*, London: Continuum.

tigertigerburning4 (2008) 'Luka Magnotta SEXIEST MAN ALIVE'. *YouTube.com*. Available at: https://www.youtube.com/watch?v=q__4VE1zzs8&t=31s (accessed: 30 January 2022).

Tingle, Will (2012) 'Snuff – Will's Review'. Video Nasty a Week. Available at: http://weeklynasty.blogspot.com/2012/08/ (accessed: 20 June 2019).

Tzioumakis, Yannis (2006) *American Independent Cinema*. Edinburgh: Edinburgh University Press.

Ward, Glenn (2009) 'Made in South America: Locating Snuff', in Ruétalo, Victoria and Tierney, Dolores. (eds) *Latsploitation, Exploitation Cinemas, and Latin America*. London: Routledge.

Walker, Samuel (1999) *In Defence of American Liberties: History of the A.C.L.U*. Carbondale, IL: Southern Illinois University Press.

Walker, Johnny (2016) 'Traces of Snuff: Black Markets, Fan Subcultures, and Underground Horror in the 1990s', in Jackson, Neil et al. (eds) *Snuff: Real Death and Screen Media*. London: Bloomsbury. pp. 137-152.

Walker, Johnny (2022) *Rewind, Replay. Britain and the Video Boom, 1978-92*. Edinburgh: Edinburgh University Press.

West, Alex (2020) 'UNRELEASED TAPES I hunted Don't F**k With Cats psycho Luka Magnotta – listen to the moment I confronted him 6 months before he killed'. *The Sun*. Available at: https://www.thesun.co.uk/news/10803623/unreleased-tapes-luka-magnotta-dont-with-cats-killer (accessed: January 2022).

Wells, Tom, West, Alex (2012) 'Cannibal on run after warning The Sun: I can't stop killing'. *The Sun*. Archived from the original on June 12, 2018. Retrieved 8 June, 2018.

Williams, Linda (1989) 'Power, Pleasure, and Perversion: Sadomasochistic Film Pornography', *Representations*, No. 27 (Summer, 1989), pp. 37-65.

Wittern-Keller, Laura and Haberski, Jr., Raymond J. (2008) *The Miracle Case: Film Censorship and the Supreme Court*. Lawrence, KS: University Press of Kansas.

Filmography

8mm (1976) Directed by Schumacher, Joel [Feature film]. Sony Pictures Releasing.

A Clockwork Orange (1971) Directed by Kubrick, Stanley [Feature film]. Warner Bros.

A Serbian Film (2010) Directed by Spasojević, Srđan [Feature film]. Unearthed Films.

August Underground's Mordum (2003) Directed by Vogel, Fred [Feature film]. Toetag Pictures.

The Beast in Heat (1977) Directed by Batzella, Luigi [Feature film]. Indipendenti Regionali.

Behind the Green Door (1972) Directed by Mitchell, Artie & Mitchell, Jim [Feature film]. Mitchell Brothers Film Group.

The Best of Sex and Violence (1982) Directed by Dixon, Ken [Feature film]. Wizard Video.

Blood Feast (1963) Directed by Gordon Lewis, Herschell [Feature film]. Box Office Spectaculars.

Blue Movie (1969) Directed by Warhol, Andy [Feature film]. Andy Warhol Films.

Body of a Female (1964) Directed by Findlay, Michael [Feature film]. Joseph Brenner Associates.

Cannibal Holocaust (1980) Directed by Deodato, Ruggero [Feature film]. United Artists Europa.

The Curse of Her Flesh (1968) Directed by Findlay, Michael [Feature film]. American Film Distributing Corporation.

Death Trap (1976) Directed by Hooper, Tobe. [Feature film]. Distributor unknown.

The Debauchers (1970) Directed by Knight, Sydney [Feature film]. Distributor unknown.

Deep Throat (1973) Directed by Damiano, Gerard [Feature film]. Bryanston Distributing Company.

The Devil in Miss Jones (1973) Directed by Damiano, Gerard [Feature film]. VCX Ltd.

The Devil's Rain (1976) Directed by Fuest, Robert [Feature film]. Bryanston Distributing Company.

The Devil's Rejects (2005) Directed by Zombie, Rob [Feature film]. Lionsgate Films.

The Driller Killer (1979) Directed by Ferrara, Abel [Feature film]. Rochelle Films.

Easy Rider (1969) Directed by Hopper, Dennis [Feature film]. Columbia Pictures.

Faces of Death (1978) Directed by Schwartz, John Alan [Feature film]. Aquarius Releasing.

Fantastic Invasion of Planet Earth (1966) Directed by Oboler, Arch [Feature film]. Monarch Releasing Corporation.

Forced Entry (1973) Directed by Costello, Shaun [Feature film]. Variety Films.

Garden of Eden (1954) Directed by Nosseck, Max [Feature film]. Excelsior Pictures Corp.

The Girl on a Motorcycle (1969) Directed by Cardiff, Jack [Feature film]. British Lion Films.

Guinea Pig: Flower of Flesh and Blood (1985) Directed by Hino, Hideshi. [Feature film]. Distributor unknown.

Hardcore (1976) Directed by Schrader, Paul [Feature film]. Columbia Pictures.

Hostel (2005) Directed by Roth, Eli [Feature film]. Lionsgate Films.

Hungry Bitches (2007) Directed by Fiorito, Marco [Feature film]. MFX Media.

I Spit on Your Grave (1978) Directed by Zarchi, Meir [Feature film]. The Jerry Gross Organisation.

The Immoral Mr Teas (1959) Directed by Meyer, Russ [Feature film]. Pad-Ram Enterprises.

In the Realm of the Senses (1976) Directed by Ōshima, Nagisa [Feature film]. Argos Films

The Kiss of Her Flesh (1968) Directed by Findlay, Michael [Feature film]. American Film Distributing Corporation.

L'Amore (1948) Directed by Rossellini, Roberto [Feature film]. Joseph Burstyn.

Love Camp 7 (1969) Directed by Frost, Lee [Feature film]. Olympic International Films.

The Language of Love (1969) Directed by Wickman, Torgny [Documentary]. Unknown.

La Ronde (1950) Directed by Ophüls, Max [Feature film]. Distributor unknown.

The Man Who Shot Liberty Valance (1962) Directed by Ford, John [Feature film]. Paramount Pictures.

'Never Gonna Give You Up' (1987) Directed by West, Simon [Music video]. PWL.

Olga's House of Shame (1964) Directed by Mawra, Joseph P. [Feature film]. Unknown.

The Opening of Misty Beethoven (1976) Directed by Metzger, Radley [Feature film]. Catalyst Productions.

The Passion of the Christ (2004) Directed by Gibson, Mel [Feature film]. Icon Productions.

Pretty Baby (1978) Directed by Malle, Louis [Feature film]. Paramount Pictures.

Race with the Devil (1975) Directed by Starrett, Jack [Feature Film]. 20th Century Fox.

Revenge of Cheerleaders (1976) Directed by Lerner, Richard [Feature Film]. Monarch Releasing Corporation.

Salò (1975) Directed by Pasolini, Pier Paolo [Feature film]. United Artists.

Satan's Bed (1965) Directed by Findlay, Michael [Feature film]. Prometheus Ventures Inc.

Saw (2004) Directed by Wan, James. [Feature film]. Lionsgate Films.

Scum of the Earth! (1963) Directed by Gordon Lewis, Herschell [Feature film]. Box Office Spectaculars

She-Devils on Wheels (1968) Directed by Gordon Lewis, Herschell [Feature film]. Mayflower Pictures.

Snuff (1976) Directed by Findlay, Michael [Feature film]. Monarch Releasing Corporation.

The Slaughter (1971) Directed by Findlay, Michael [Feature film]. Never released.

Slaughtered Vomit Dolls (2006) Directed by Valentine, Lucifer [Feature film]. Unearthed Films.

The Slasher (1972) Directed by Montero, Roberto Bianchi [Feature film]. Monarch Releasing Corporation.

SS Experiment Camp (1976) Directed by Garrone, Sergio. [Feature film]. Distributor unknown.

Straw Dogs (1971) Directed by Peckinpah, Sam [Feature film]. 20th Century Fox

The Story of O (1975) Directed by Jaeckin, Just [Feature film]. S.N. Prodis.

Touch of Her Flesh (1967) Directed by Findlay, Michael [Feature film]. American Film

Distributing Corporation.

Traces of Death (1993) Directed by Fox, Damon [Documentary]. Brain Damage Films.

Water Power (1976) Directed by Costello, Shaun [Feature film]. Star Distributors.

White Slaves of Chinatown (1964) Directed by Mawra, Joseph P. [Feature film]. Unknown.

Wolf Creek (2005) Directed by McLean, Greg [Feature film]. Roadshow Entertainment.

TELEVISION

The Dark Side of Porn (2006). Season 2, episode 4 (dir. Barry, Evy).

Masters of Horror (2005). Season 1, episode 8 (dir. Carpenter, John).

Inside Number 9 (2016). Season 3, episode 1 (dir. Harper, Graeme).

www.ingramcontent.com/pod-product-compliance
Lightning Source LLC
Chambersburg PA
CBHW070734230426
43665CB00016B/2243